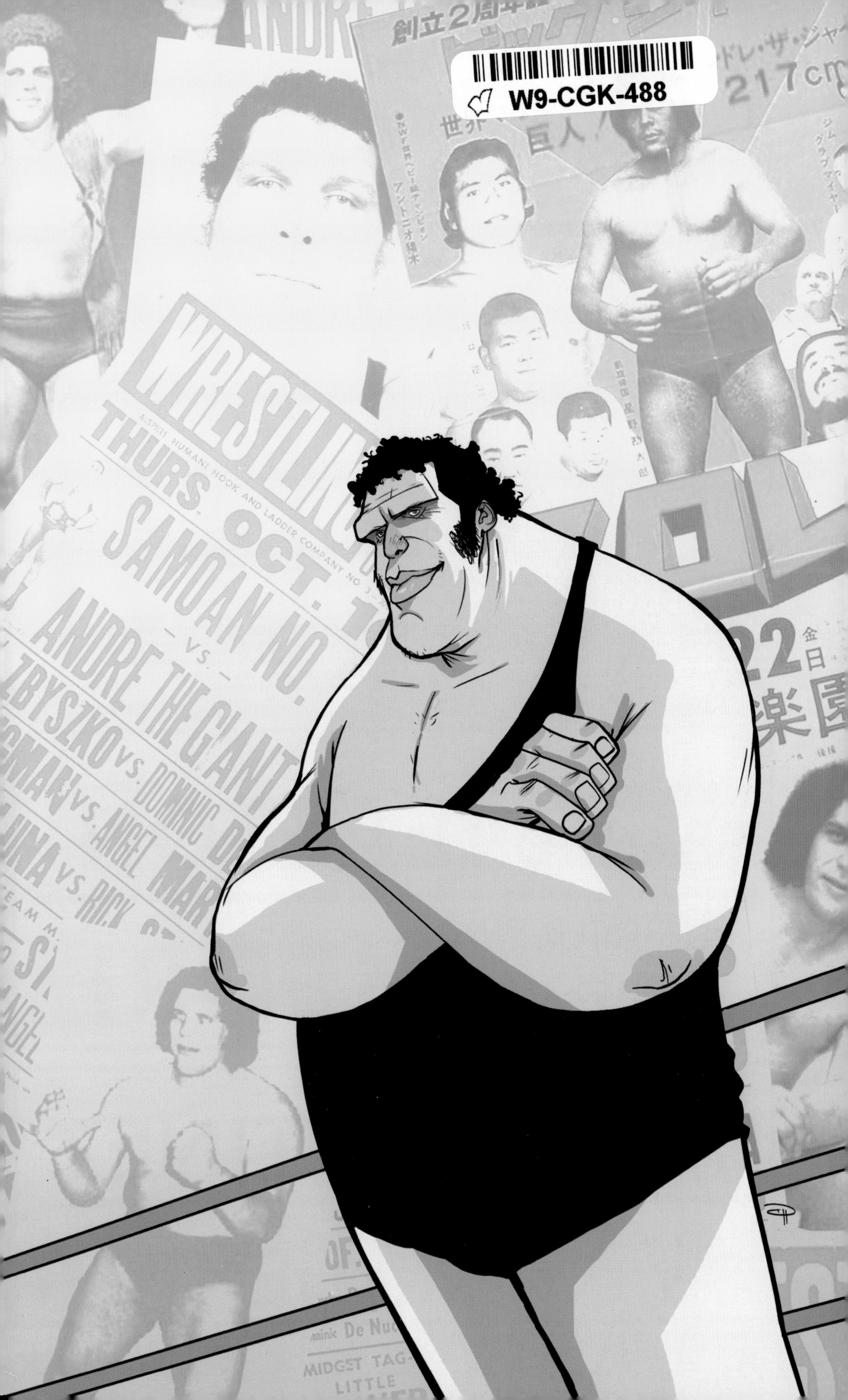

創立2周年記
217cm
巨人
WRESTLING
AUSPICES HUMANE HOOK AND LADDER COMPANY NO. 3
THURS. OCT. 1
SAMOAN NO.
— VS. —
ANDRE THE GIANT
ZBYSZKO VS. DOMINIC D
VS. ANGEL MAR
VS. RICK
22 金 日
楽園
minic De Nuc
MIDGET TAG-
LITTLE

WRESTLING S

Trophy Night Kno

ANDRE

★ ★ ★ -VS

WRITTEN BY
Eisner Nominee
BRANDON **EASTON**

ILLUSTRATED BY
DENIS **MEDRI**

LETTERED BY
AW's ADRIAN **MARTINEZ**

BOOK DESIGN
KRISTEN FITZNER **DENTON**

PECTACULAR

k-Out Tournament

the GIANT

André Roussimoff

COLORED BY
DAVIDE CACI

EDITED BY **SHANNON ERIC**
DENTON

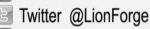

 Facebook.com/LionForge
Twitter @LionForge
YouTube.com/LionForge

ISBN: 978-1-63140-400-9

LIONFORGE.com

FOREWORD

From as early as I can remember, I knew my father was a celebrity. Although he wasn't in my life, I could see him whenever I wanted. On TV, in magazines, even in movies - Andre the Giant's public persona seemed to be everywhere. But I barely knew the man that Andre Roussimoff was when there were no cameras, fans or crowds around.

One of my earliest memories of my father was a surprise visit he made to my daycare. I must've been about four years old. My teacher must've had an interesting sight, a huge mountain of a man in a room full of tiny children. But his visits with me would be scarce, since his profession had always consumed his life. He didn't belong to me or even my mother, though they were together for seven years - despite rumors to the contrary. He belonged to the media and to professional wrestling, which kept him on the road nonstop. And sadly, his illness and personal struggles with alcohol made it even more difficult for him to be the father he may have wanted to be.

But unlike most kids who grow up without a father, I could connect with my dad in other ways. My mother brought me to see The Princess Bride. When the character of Fezzik appeared on screen I yelled out "That's my dad!" in the crowded theater. I was so excited, my mother had to pop her hand over my mouth.

Soon after that I went to see him at one of his wrestling matches. I sat on his lap, and this giant man who fought other large men for a living was trying his hardest to find common ground with an 8-year-old girl. He wanted to take an interest in my life, things like my gymnastics lessons or the music that I liked. And then he disappeared to go on the road again. Being Andre the Giant's daughter was a fact I soon learned to keep to myself. If I told people they would accuse me of lying. If they believed me, they would try to use me as a connection to him.

The last time I spoke to my father was the Christmas before he died. During the phone call I thanked him for my gift. Once again, he tried to connect with me. Making small talk about whether it would snow for the holidays - we lived in Washington where it never did. He always asked about my hobbies and interests, things a dad should know. No matter how violent he was in the ring, I'll forever remember him as a sweet man who always had a smile for me. But as the book details, I was able to write him a letter expressing my frustration at his lack of involvement in my life. It was the only closure I would ever have.

A few months later, we came home to find a message from my father's lawyer on the answering machine with the news that my dad had passed away. He wanted us to know before the media ran the story. I was just 13 years old. Maybe had he lived longer, I might have had a closer relationship with him. Perhaps he would've attended my graduation, or been proud of my successes. I'll never get to really know who he really was as a person, as opposed to the identity that the media and his employers manufactured for him.

What struck me when reading this graphic novel was the honest way it portrayed my father - not as just the wrestler or actor, but as the human being. He made mistakes and had many struggles in his life. I hope this book helps people realize that Andre the Giant was just a man who did the best he could do. Brandon Easton, the author, also portrayed my relationship with my father in one of the most truthful ways I've seen.

My mother and I were at the center of many rumors and outright lies. It was refreshing to see the truth about us instead of a storyline conceived to sell more tickets. Since my mother had a difficult time talking about my father, many parts of his private life are still a mystery to me. I hope when people read this graphic novel, they will get answers not only to who Andre the Giant was as an entertainer, but who Andre Roussimoff was as a person.

-Robin Christensen Roussimoff,
daughter of Andre "The Giant" Roussimoff

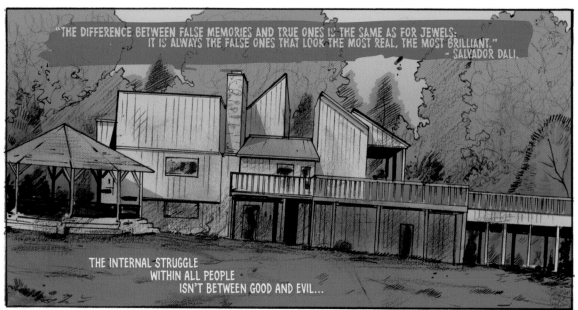

"THE DIFFERENCE BETWEEN FALSE MEMORIES AND TRUE ONES IS THE SAME AS FOR JEWELS: IT IS ALWAYS THE FALSE ONES THAT LOOK THE MOST REAL, THE MOST BRILLIANT."
— SALVADOR DALI.

THE INTERNAL STRUGGLE WITHIN ALL PEOPLE ISN'T BETWEEN GOOD AND EVIL...

...IT'S BETWEEN OPTIMISM AND PESSIMISM.

I LEARNED THIS LESSON FAR TOO LATE IN LIFE.

I'VE HEARD THAT A PESSIMIST BELIEVES THAT MEMORIES ARE ONLY REGRETS ORGANIZED IN CHRONOLOGICAL ORDER ...

...THE OPTIMIST SAYS THAT YOU SHOULD BE LUCKY TO LIVE LONG ENOUGH TO HAVE REGRETS.

1992

LORD KNOWS, THERE'S BEEN A LOT OF PAIN.

AND LORD KNOWS HOW OFTEN I'VE SMILED THROUGH IT.

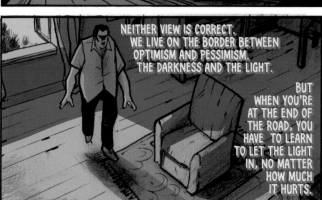

NEITHER VIEW IS CORRECT. WE LIVE ON THE BORDER BETWEEN OPTIMISM AND PESSIMISM. THE DARKNESS AND THE LIGHT.

BUT WHEN YOU'RE AT THE END OF THE ROAD, YOU HAVE TO LEARN TO LET THE LIGHT IN, NO MATTER HOW MUCH IT HURTS.

MAY 19, 1946

I WAS THE THIRD CHILD OF FIVE.

THE MIDDLE KID.

WE LIVED IN MOLIEN, FRANCE. SOME CONSIDERED IT A COMMUNE, BUT MY FATHER TURNED THE LAND INTO A SUBSISTENCE FARM.

OUR FAMILY NEVER WENT HUNGRY.

I LOVED MY FAMILY. THEY WERE MY ENTIRE WORLD. I NEVER COMPLAINED ABOUT THE ONES GOD SENT TO ME. THEY WERE A GIFT.

BUT ALL THINGS MUST CHANGE, AND WITH THE PASSAGE OF TIME, I NEEDED TO BUILD SOCIAL BONDS OUTSIDE OF MY FAMILY.

I SOON LEARNED TO LOVE SCHOOL AS MUCH AS I LOVED MY FAMILY.

IT WAS A PARADISE FOR THE OPTIMIST IN ME.

AND WHO COULD BLAME ME?

I HAD NO OTHER EXPERIENCE, NO BAROMETER OF NEGATIVITY TO JUDGE ANYTHING.

THE PASSAGE OF TIME ALSO CHANGES PRIORITIES...

DEDE...

THAT WAS MY NICKNAME... "DEDE." MY LITTLE SISTER USED TO CALL ME THAT. MY PARENTS HAD A CERTAIN TONE, THE WAY THEY PRONOUNCED THE SYLLABLES, THAT LET ME KNOW BAD NEWS WAS ON THE WAY.

...I NEED YOU TO STOP GOING TO SCHOOL. HELP ME AND YOUR BROTHER WORK THE LAND. THINGS ARE GETTING TOUGH IN THE WORLD. WE NEED ANOTHER HAND AROUND HERE.

YES SIR...

I NEVER SAW MOST OF MY CLASSMATES AGAIN.

TIME PASSED...

BY THE AGE OF TWELVE, I WAS SIX-FEET-TALL.

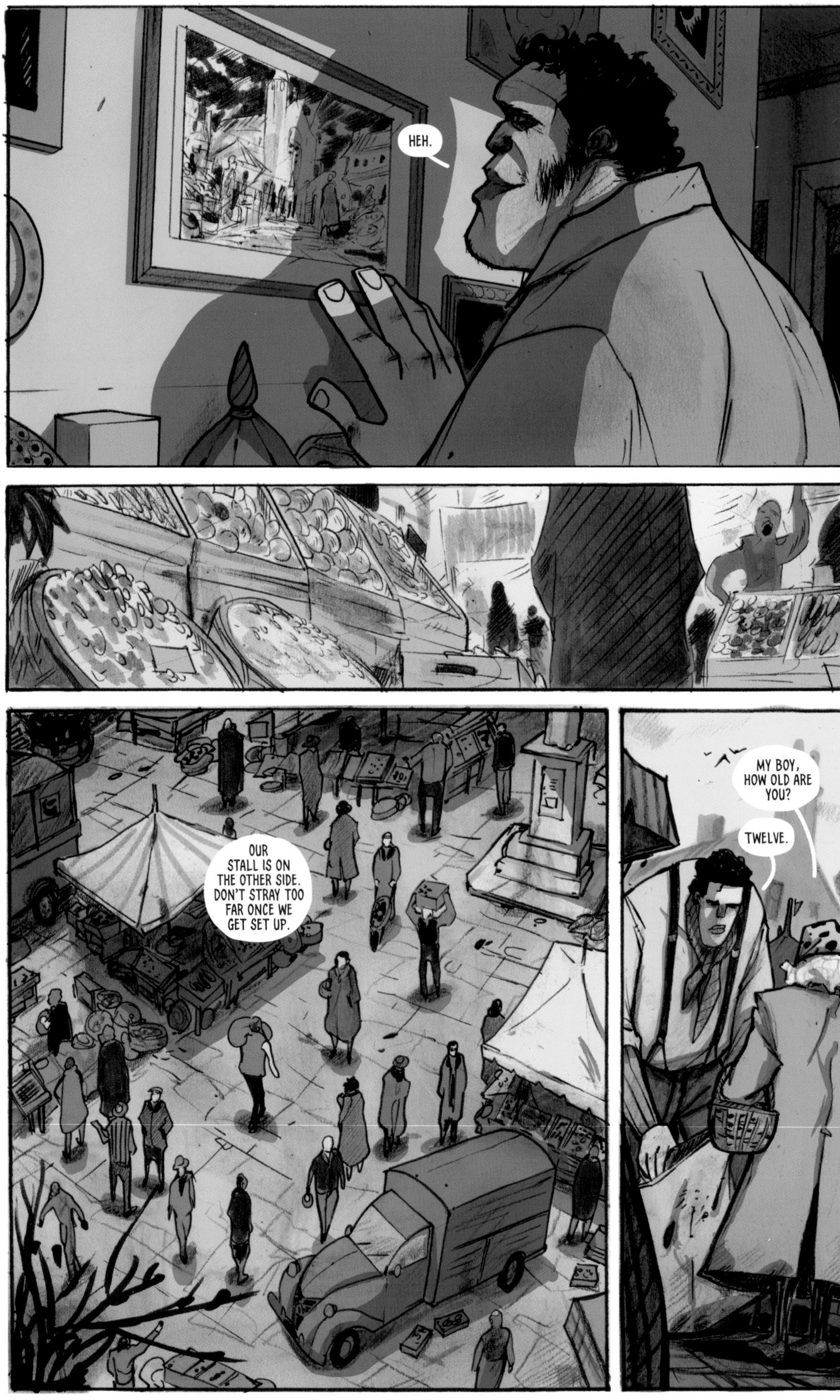
HEH.
OUR STALL IS ON THE OTHER SIDE. DON'T STRAY TOO FAR ONCE WE GET SET UP.
MY BOY, HOW OLD ARE YOU?
TWELVE.

MERCY, YOU'RE JUST A BABY.

MUST GET TIRED OF PEOPLE STARING AT YOU ALL THE TIME?

NO MA'AM. I'M USED TO IT.

IT'S NOTHING TO BE ASHAMED OF... THAT JUST MEANS THAT YOU'RE CLOSER TO HEAVEN.

THE LORD HIMSELF COULD REACH DOWN AND TAP YOU ON THE HEAD IF HE WANTED.

YES MA'AM.

WHAT THAT LADY SAID MADE A LOT OF SENSE, IF YOU WERE ONE BEHOLDEN TO DEEP FAITH. I WAS TALLER THAN EVERYONE ELSE... BUT WHETHER THAT MADE ME "CLOSER TO HEAVEN" OR JUST A FREAK OF NATURE WAS A TRUTH I'D HAVE TO DISCOVER ON MY OWN.

AS TIME PASSED, I CONTINUED TO GROW LARGER...

...AND LARGER...

...AND LARGER.

I BEGAN TO WONDER IF I WAS GOING TO OUTGROW THE WORLD ITSELF.

I HAD TO MAKE A DECISION... THE FARM NO LONGER FIT.

I NEEDED TO LEAVE.

I HAD TO FIND MYSELF. FIGURE OUT WHERE I BELONGED AND IF THERE WAS SUCH A PLACE ANYWHERE ON EARTH.

I DIGRESS...

THERE WAS ONE PLACE

WHERE I FELT AT HOME,

REGARDLESS OF MY SIZE.

I LOVED GOING TO THE WRESTLING MATCHES. ALL THE FRENCH BOYS LOVED WATCHING "LE CATCH" AS WE CALLED IT.

IT WAS SAID FRENCH BOYS GOT EXCITED ABOUT THREE THINGS: WOMEN, FOOTBALL, AND LE CATCH.

I MET A LOCAL WRESTLING PROMOTER. HE FELT THAT WE SHOULD WORK TOGETHER.

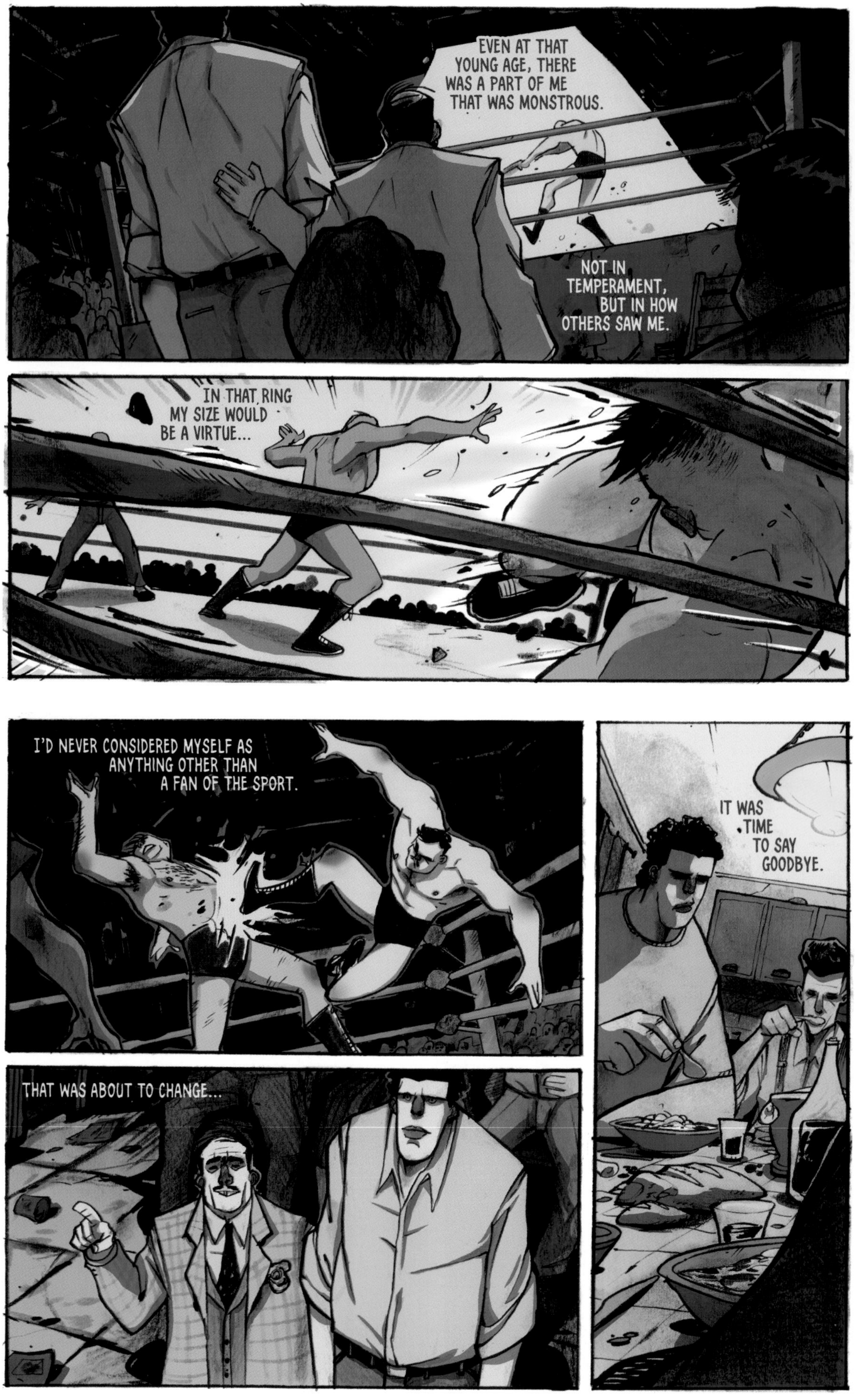
EVEN AT THAT YOUNG AGE, THERE WAS A PART OF ME THAT WAS MONSTROUS.
NOT IN TEMPERAMENT, BUT IN HOW OTHERS SAW ME.
IN THAT RING MY SIZE WOULD BE A VIRTUE...
I'D NEVER CONSIDERED MYSELF AS ANYTHING OTHER THAN A FAN OF THE SPORT.
THAT WAS ABOUT TO CHANGE...
IT WAS TIME TO SAY GOODBYE.

THOSE OUTSIDE OF THE SPORT OFTEN CONFUSE THE PREDETERMINED OUTCOME WITH AN ABSENCE OF PAIN.

FRANK...

KNOWING THE OUTCOME RARELY REDUCES HOW MUCH IT HURTS...

...AND WHEN YOU TAKE THE FIRST STEP ONTO A PATH OF GLORY, THE LIGHT BLINDS YOU TO EVERYTHING.

THE TRUE ART OF PROFESSIONAL WRESTLING IS TO SIMULATE VIOLENCE AND TRANSFORM IT INTO THEATER.

THE MOMENT YOU STEP INTO THE RING YOU HAVE TO TRUST THE OTHER GUY TO NOT KILL YOU. NO ONE TRIES TO HARM YOU ON PURPOSE, BUT ALL IT TAKES IS A MISPLACED STEP OR A HARD THRUST, AND A MAN COULD DIE IN AN INSTANT.

THE FIRST TRICKS YOU LEARN ARE "STAND UP" TECHNIQUES. ANYONE CAN TOSS A PUNCH OR A KICK, BUT THE AUDIENCE HAS TO BUY THE MUTUAL AGGRESSION OF THE OPPONENTS. THE COLLAR-AND-ELBOW TIE-UP IS THE FIRST MOVE YOU LEARN. THEY MADE ME REPEAT THIS HUNDREDS OF TIMES. AFTER AN HOUR, I COULDN'T FEEL MY UPPER BODY.

LEARNING HOW TO FALL IS THE KEY TO THE SUSPENSION OF DISBELIEF IN THE RING. A WRESTLER HAS TO UNLEARN SELF-PRESERVATION.

TUCK YOUR CHIN INTO YOUR CHEST, SPREAD YOUR ARMS AND SHOULDERS AND FALL ONTO THE CENTER OF YOUR BACK.

WHEN YOU HIT THE MAT, THE NOISE WILL ECHO ACROSS THE ARENA. IT SOUNDS WORSE THAN IT IS. BUT IT'S GONNA STING NO MATTER WHAT!

WHAP

SORRY.

1963

AND SO IT BEGAN...

THE WINNER OF THIS MATCH... GÉANT FERRE!!!

WHOOM!

1— 2— 3!!!

MATCH AFTER MATCH THE CROWDS GREW LARGER...

...AS DID MY NAME.

THE WINNER OF THIS MATCH... MONSTER EIFFEL TOWER!!!

INCREDIBLE.

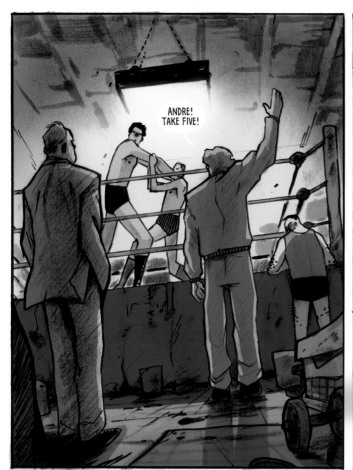

ANDRE! TAKE FIVE!

ANDRE, I WANT YOU TO MEET MY FRIEND **FRANK VALOIS**. HE'S A PROMOTER FROM NORTH AMERICA.

MERCI.

BONJOUR. YOU'RE IMPRESSIVE.

YOU EVER GET TIRED OF PEOPLE STARING?

USED TO IT. CAN'T BE A PERFORMER UNLESS PEOPLE WANT TO STARE.

GOOD POINT. LET'S CUT TO THE POINT. I'VE NEVER SEEN ANYONE LIKE YOU BEFORE AND I'VE BEEN TO EVERY CORNER OF THE EARTH.

PEOPLE SAY THAT TO ME ALL THE TIME. WHAT ARE YOU SELLING?

THE DIFFERENCE BETWEEN ME AND ALL THE HUCKSTERS OUT THERE IS THAT I HAVE A THIRTY-EIGHT-YEAR CAREER UNDER MY BELT.

I KNOW *THINGS* ABOUT THE WRESTLING GAME... THINGS THAT COULD MAKE US BOTH LOTS OF MONEY.

HOW SO?

I WASN'T KIDDING ABOUT MY GLOBAL EXPOSURE. I'VE GOT CONNECTIONS WITH WRESTLING TERRITORIES BEYOND EUROPE. I'M TALKING ASIA, THE SOUTH PACIFIC, AUSTRALIA... EVEN THE AFRICAN CONTINENT.

YOU STAY LOCAL, YOU MAKE A FEW MORE BUCKS. YOU GO WITH ME, THERE'S MILLIONS ON THE TABLE. WHAT DO YOU SAY?

SURE THING... BOSS.

"BOSS?" I LIKE THE SOUND OF THAT.

IT WAS 1966. FRANK VALOIS BECAME MY BUSINESS MANAGER. AND HE MADE GOOD ON HIS PROMISE. I WENT FROM BEING A EUROPEAN ATTRACTION TO A GLOBAL SUPERSTAR.

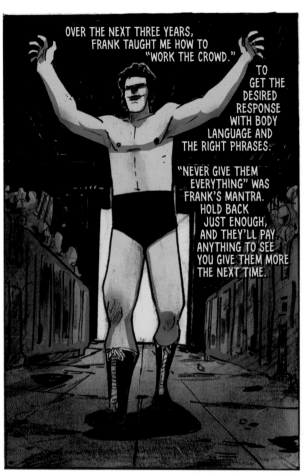

OVER THE NEXT THREE YEARS, FRANK TAUGHT ME HOW TO "WORK THE CROWD."

TO GET THE DESIRED RESPONSE WITH BODY LANGUAGE AND THE RIGHT PHRASES:

"NEVER GIVE THEM EVERYTHING" WAS FRANK'S MANTRA. HOLD BACK JUST ENOUGH, AND THEY'LL PAY ANYTHING TO SEE YOU GIVE THEM MORE THE NEXT TIME.

HE WAS RIGHT.

BOY, WAS HE RIGHT.

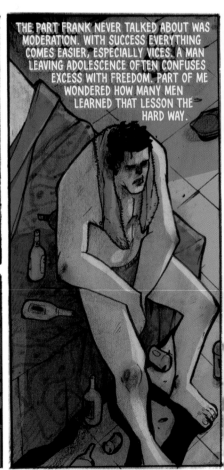

THE PART FRANK NEVER TALKED ABOUT WAS MODERATION. WITH SUCCESS EVERYTHING COMES EASIER, ESPECIALLY VICES. A MAN LEAVING ADOLESCENCE OFTEN CONFUSES EXCESS WITH FREEDOM. PART OF ME WONDERED HOW MANY MEN LEARNED THAT LESSON THE HARD WAY.

THERE WERE THINGS I WAS PREPARED FOR...

AND A FEW NEW SITUATIONS THAT WERE WELCOME DISTRACTIONS.

BEHIND THE SCENES,
THERE IS A CULTURE OF DEBAUCHERY
THAT IS EXCUSED BECAUSE
"BOYS WILL BE BOYS."

NO MATTER WHAT WE DID,
IT WAS FORGIVEN UNDER
THE UMBRELLA OF BEING
ONE OF THE "BOYS."

POP!

GURGLE.

SLOSH.

⸾BURP⸾
...GOT
ANY MORE?

IN A
WORLD
WITH NO
LIMITS, TEMPTATION
CEASES TO EXIST.
IT IS REPLACED
WITH ROUTINE.

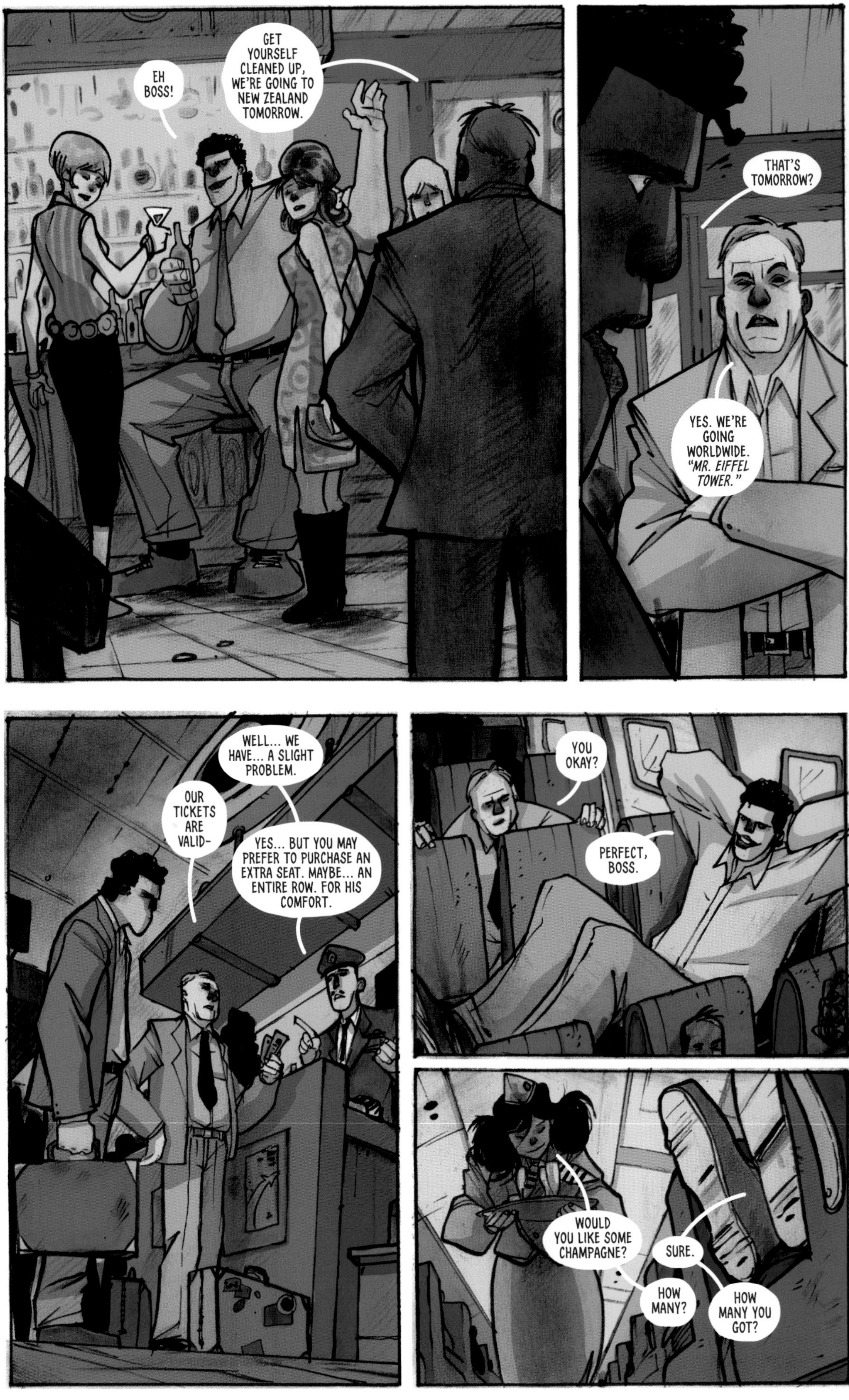
EH BOSS!
GET YOURSELF CLEANED UP, WE'RE GOING TO NEW ZEALAND TOMORROW.
THAT'S TOMORROW?
YES. WE'RE GOING WORLDWIDE. *"MR. EIFFEL TOWER."*
OUR TICKETS ARE VALID-
WELL... WE HAVE... A SLIGHT PROBLEM.
YES... BUT YOU MAY PREFER TO PURCHASE AN EXTRA SEAT. MAYBE... AN ENTIRE ROW. FOR HIS COMFORT.
YOU OKAY?
PERFECT, BOSS.
WOULD YOU LIKE SOME CHAMPAGNE?
SURE.
HOW MANY?
HOW MANY YOU GOT?

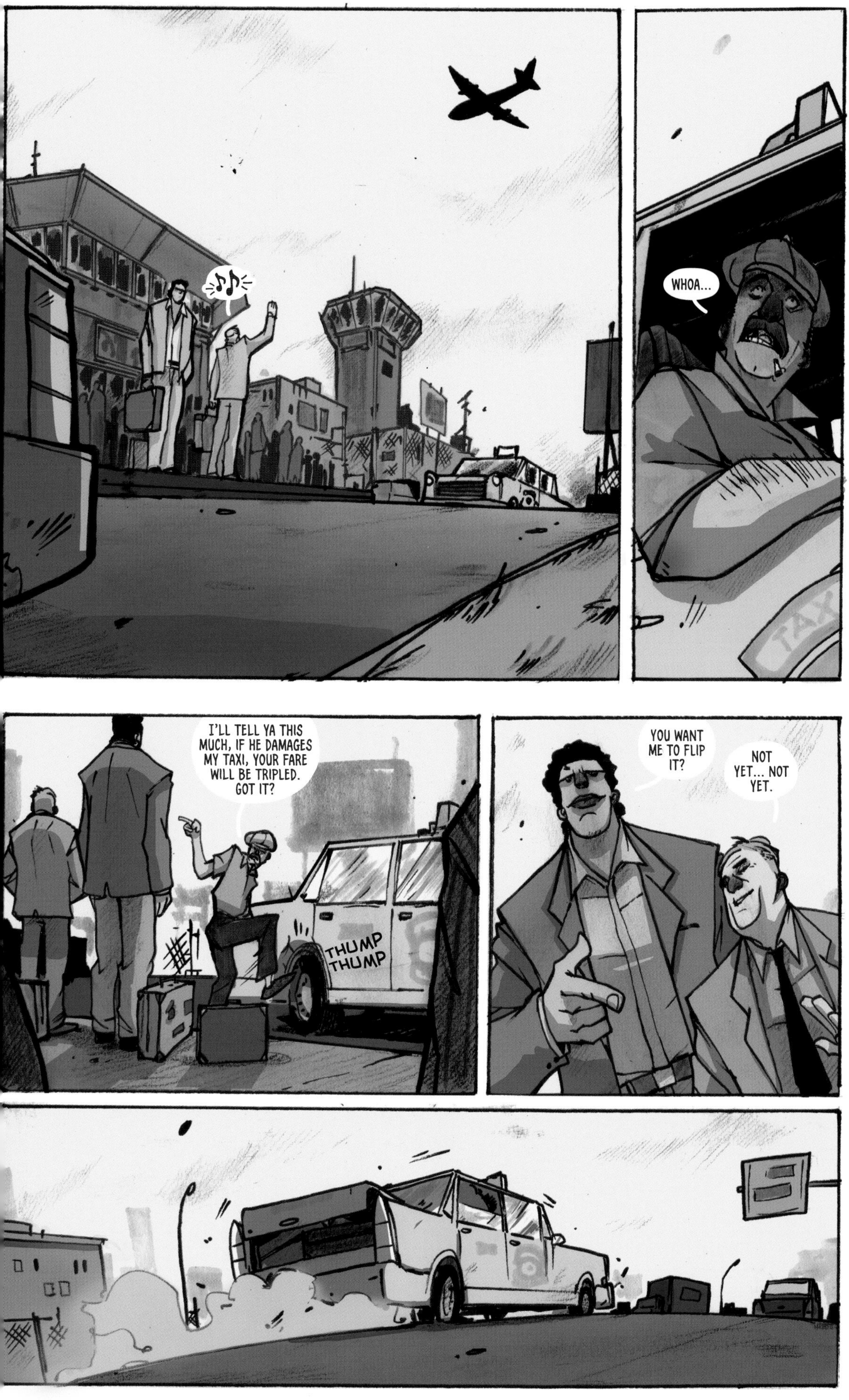
WHOA...
I'LL TELL YA THIS MUCH, IF HE DAMAGES MY TAXI, YOUR FARE WILL BE TRIPLED. GOT IT?
THUMP THUMP
YOU WANT ME TO FLIP IT?
NOT YET... NOT YET.

FOR A WHILE,
MY SIZE WAS ENOUGH TO DRAW A CROWD,
BUT FRANK AND I KNEW THAT I WAS
GOING TO HAVE TO BROADEN MY
MOVE-SET SOONER OR LATER.

FWOOOSH!

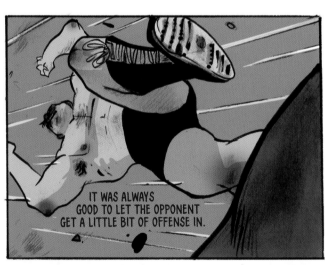

IT WAS ALWAYS
GOOD TO LET THE OPPONENT
GET A LITTLE BIT OF OFFENSE IN.

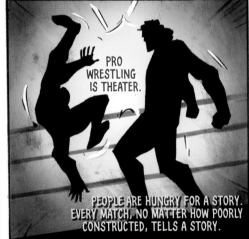

PRO
WRESTLING
IS THEATER.

PEOPLE ARE HUNGRY FOR A STORY.
EVERY MATCH, NO MATTER HOW POORLY
CONSTRUCTED, TELLS A STORY.

MY STORY WAS ALWAYS
"DAVID VS. GOLIATH"
EXCEPT THAT GOLIATH
WAS THE HERO.

WHAMMMMM!

1—
2—
3!!

FRANK TOLD ME THAT
MY DAYS OF SHOWBOATING WOULD
HAVE TO END IF WE WERE GOING
TO CONQUER THE TOUGHEST
PRO WRESTLING SCENE
IN THE WORLD...

JAPAN.

AFTER WORLD WAR II, PRO WRESTLING – BETTER KNOWN AS PURORESU OR PURO – BECAME A SUCCESSFUL FORM OF ENTERTAINMENT.

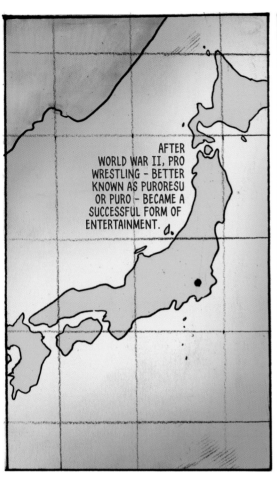

RIKIDOZAN GAINED PROMINENCE DURING A TIME WHEN THE JAPANESE NATIONAL SPIRIT WAS DAMAGED AFTER THE DEVASTATION OF HIROSHIMA AND NAGASAKI. HE APPEALED TO THE DESIRES OF THE JAPANESE FANS WHO DESPERATELY WANTED TO SEE A PROUD NATIONAL HERO "STAND UP" TO THE AMERICANS.

RIKIDOZAN AND HIS PEERS DEVELOPED A STYLE OF WRESTLING THAT EMPHASIZED THE SKILL OF THE OPPONENTS INSTEAD OF PURELY THEATRICAL STORYTELLING.

MATCHES ARE TREATED AS LEGITIMATE FIGHTS WITH FULL-CONTACT MARTIAL ARTS BLOWS AND A PACE THAT REQUIRES ALMOST SUPERHUMAN LEVELS OF ENDURANCE.

FRANK BOOKED ME IN THE NUMBER ONE FEDERATION IN JAPAN – *INTERNATIONAL WRESTLING ENTERPRISE* – FOR A TOUR.

THE OWNER, ISAO YOSHIHARA, WAS CERTAIN I WOULD MAKE AN IMPACT ON THE SCENE.

HE HAD NO IDEA HOW BIG.

JAN 18 1970

‹THE WINNERS OF THIS MATCH...›

‹AND THE NEW IWE WORLD TAG TEAM CHAMPIONS... *MICHAEL NADOR AND MONSTER ROUSSIMOFF!*›

IT WAS ON THE FLOOR OF THE JAPANESE PURORESU DOJOS THAT I LEARNED THE IMPORTANCE OF INCORPORATING TECHNICAL ASPECTS INTO MY MATCHES.

FRANK ALWAYS EMPHASIZED FINDING NEW WAYS TO MAXIMIZE MY VALUE AS A PERFORMER. IN JAPAN, YOU HAD TO BE MORE THAN A MONSTER, YOU HAD TO BE A MONSTER WHO COULD OUT-WRESTLE A HOMEGROWN HERO.

FOR EXAMPLE...

WHAAMMM O!

SEE, BOSS... LEAVE 'EM WANTING MORE.

A FEW DAYS LATER...

HEY!

...

BOSS?

COME WITH ME, ANDRE.

WHAT IS IT AGAIN...?

ACROMEGALY.

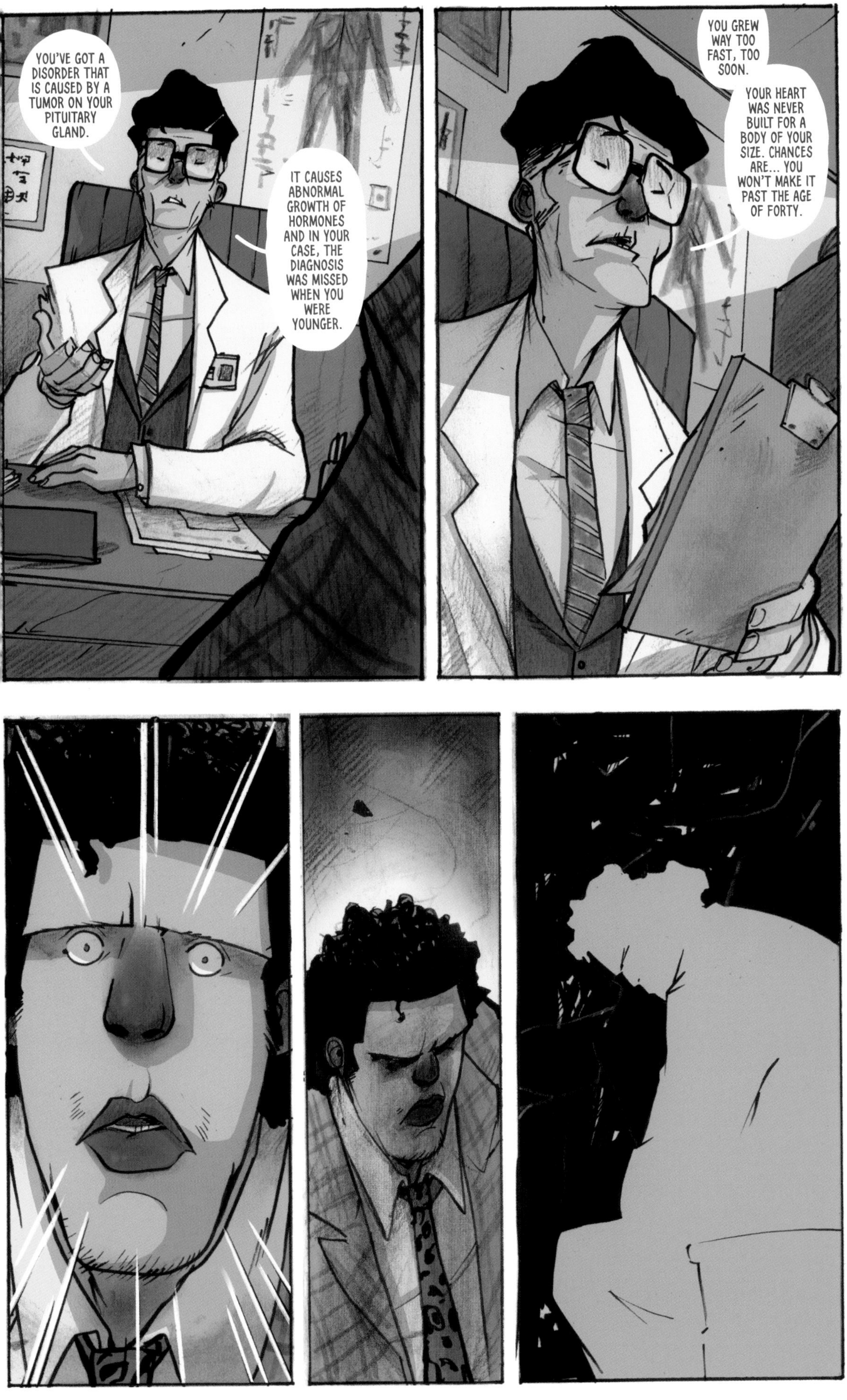
YOU'VE GOT A DISORDER THAT IS CAUSED BY A TUMOR ON YOUR PITUITARY GLAND.
IT CAUSES ABNORMAL GROWTH OF HORMONES AND IN YOUR CASE, THE DIAGNOSIS WAS MISSED WHEN YOU WERE YOUNGER.
YOU GREW WAY TOO FAST, TOO SOON.
YOUR HEART WAS NEVER BUILT FOR A BODY OF YOUR SIZE. CHANCES ARE... YOU WON'T MAKE IT PAST THE AGE OF FORTY.

ANDRE?

I'M OKAY, BOSS.

YOU DON'T HAVE TO PRETEND WITH ME—

WHAT DO I HAVE TO FEEL BAD ABOUT? LOOK AT US, WE'RE AT THE TOP OF THE WORLD.

ALL THOSE PEOPLE DOWN THERE, IT WOULD TAKE THEM TEN YEARS TO EXPERIENCE WHAT I DO IN A WEEK.

YOU HAVE A FULL LIFE AHEAD OF YOU, ANDRE. NOT ALL DOCTORS ARE RIGHT ALL OF THE TIME.

KNOCK-KNOCK!

I'VE GOT A FULL LIFE ALREADY. G'NIGHT, BOSS.

MY LEGEND WAS GROWING. THE DEMAND TO SEE ME WAS STRONG ACROSS THE GLOBE.

GRAND PRIX CATAPULTED MY CAREER IN WAYS I DIDN'T IMAGINE. WHILE I WAS ALREADY A STAR, I DIDN'T HAVE A *CHARACTER*. I PAID CLOSE ATTENTION TO MY FREQUENT TAG PARTNER ÉDOUARD CARPENTIER. I WATCHED HOW HE BECAME SOMEONE DIFFERENT IN THE RING.

PARTICULARLY IN THE FRENCH-SPEAKING PORTION OF NORTH AMERICA.

MONTREAL, QUEBEC... I'D BEEN BOOKED FOR GRAND PRIX WRESTLING AS THE "EIGHTH WONDER OF THE WORLD."

I LIKED THE SOUND OF THAT.

I HAD TO BECOME HEROIC. MORE THAN JUST A MONSTER... IN GRAND PRIX, THEY CALLED ME "JEAN FERRE."

A CRIME-FIGHTING CRUSADER ON THE SCENE TO STOP THE FORCES OF EVIL FROM PROSPERING IN THE MONTREAL TERRITORY.

TH OK!!!

ONE OF MY BIGGEST RIVALS WAS "KILLER" KOWALSKI. HE WAS ONE OF THE NICEST GUYS IN THE WORLD WHEN OUT OF CHARACTER...

...BUT IN THE RING, HE WAS THE WORST VILLAIN YOU EVER SAW. HE ONCE RIPPED YUKON ERIC'S EAR OFF IN A MATCH. OF COURSE THE GUY'S EAR WAS CAULIFLOWERED AND USELESS, BUT THE FANS DIDN'T KNOW THAT.

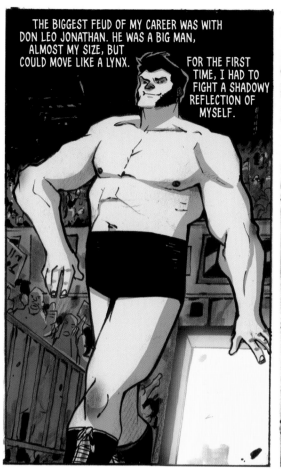

THE BIGGEST FEUD OF MY CAREER WAS WITH DON LEO JONATHAN. HE WAS A BIG MAN, ALMOST MY SIZE, BUT COULD MOVE LIKE A LYNX.

FOR THE FIRST TIME, I HAD TO FIGHT A SHADOWY REFLECTION OF MYSELF.

OUR BATTLES RAGED FOR MONTHS...

...AND THE FAN INTEREST WAS WHITE HOT.

THE HYPE WORKED... OVER TWENTY-THOUSAND FANS SHOWED UP. OUR MATCH SET CANADA'S INDOOR ATTENDANCE RECORD.

THE "MATCH OF THE CENTURY" IS HAPPENING AT THE END OF THE MONTH!

ON MAY THIRTY-FIRST, NINETEEN SEVENTY-TWO GRAND PRIX WRESTLING WILL HOST A CONTEST OF TITANS!

JEAN FERRE VERSUS THE HATED DON LEO JONATHAN.

TICKETS ARE SELLING FAST SO YOU BETTER GRAB YOURS WHILE THEY LAST. THE MONTREAL FORUM IS THE PLACE AND DON'T BE LEFT OUT! YOU WILL NEVER, AND I MEAN NEVER SEE ANYTHING LIKE THIS AGAIN!

DING! DING!

NO QUARTER WAS GIVEN...

THOOOM!

WHOK!

...NONE WAS ASKED FOR...

THE FANS BOUGHT INTO IT ONE-HUNDRED PERCENT. WITH EVERY BODY SLAM, PUNCH OR KICK, YOU'D HEAR GASPS AND SCREAMS.

THINGS WERE AT A FEVER PITCH. IT WAS TIME TO "BRING IT ON HOME" AS WE SAID IN THE BUSINESS.

EVEN IN PRO WRESTLING, THERE WERE RULES. ONE OF THE CORE RULES WAS "NO CHOKING YOUR OPPONENT."

IN THE STORY OF THIS MATCH, DON LEO'S ANTICS MADE ME LOSE MY TEMPER.

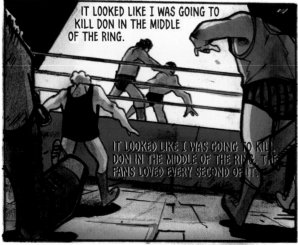

IT LOOKED LIKE I WAS GOING TO KILL DON IN THE MIDDLE OF THE RING.

IT LOOKED LIKE I WAS GOING TO KILL DON IN THE MIDDLE OF THE RING. THE FANS LOVED EVERY SECOND OF IT.

WHAT I DID NEXT CHANGED MY CAREER FOREVER...

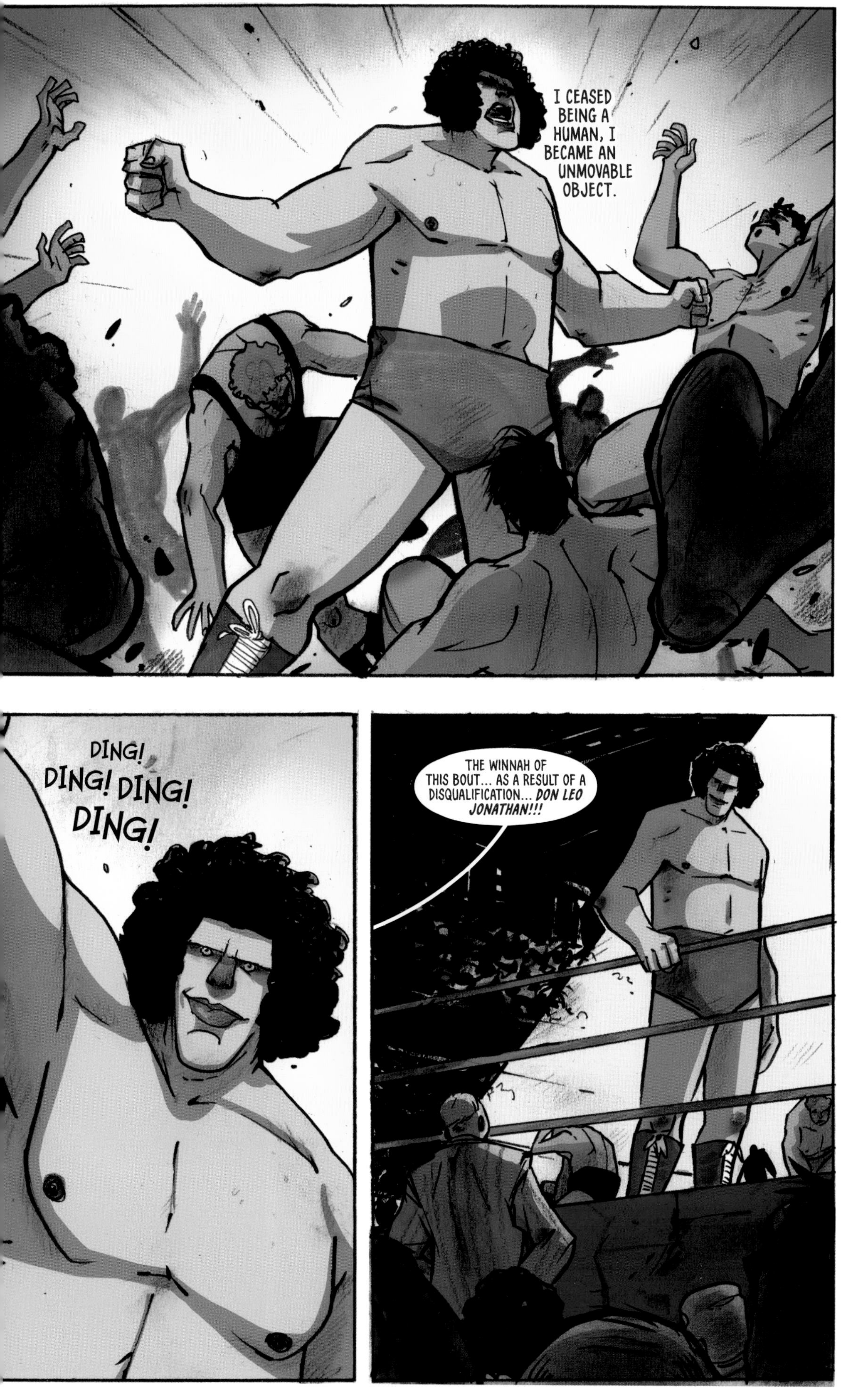
I CEASED BEING A HUMAN, I BECAME AN UNMOVABLE OBJECT.
DING! DING! DING! DING!
THE WINNAH OF THIS BOUT... AS A RESULT OF A DISQUALIFICATION... DON LEO JONATHAN!!!

AFTER THAT MATCH, MY LEGEND BECAME AS BIG AS CANADA ITSELF... BUT THERE WAS A HIDDEN COST OF BEING A SUPERHERO.

A HERO IS ONLY VALID IF THEY HAVE AN ENEMY OF EQUAL OR GREATER POWER.

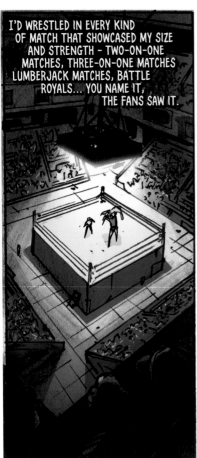

I'D WRESTLED IN EVERY KIND OF MATCH THAT SHOWCASED MY SIZE AND STRENGTH – TWO-ON-ONE MATCHES, THREE-ON-ONE MATCHES LUMBERJACK MATCHES, BATTLE ROYALS... YOU NAME IT, THE FANS SAW IT.

I RAN OUT OF VILLAINS. IN THE MONTREAL TERRITORY, FANS GREW TIRED OF WATCHING ME BEAT UP ON THE SAME GUYS OVER AND OVER AGAIN.

THE GATE RECEIPTS REVEALED THEIR LACK OF ENTHUSIASM.

AFTER A FEW YEARS OF THIS, WHO COULD BLAME THEM?

FRANK HAD BEEN ACTING STRANGE LATELY. I KNEW SOMETHING WAS UP, BUT I COULDN'T FIGURE OUT WHAT WAS UP HIS SLEEVE.

ANDRE, YOU GOT A MINUTE?

FOR YOU BOSS, ALWAYS.

WHAT'S NEXT, ANDRE?

GUUUZZZLLLE... WITH...?

SLURRRP

03

YOUR CAREER... OUR CAREER. YOU HAVE EYES, THE CROWDS AIN'T COMING TO WATCH YOU ANYMORE. THE FRESHNESS HAS WORN OFF AND THE LONGER YOU WRESTLE HERE, THE SOONER YOU'LL BE A FORGOTTEN CIRCUS FREAK.

I'M NOT STUPID. I KNOW WHAT'S HAPPENING. I FIGURED WE'D GO ON ANOTHER WORLD TOUR TO GET THINGS HEATED UP AGAIN.

SKRRNCH!

SOMETIMES THE WORLD ISN'T ENOUGH. YOU NEED TO GAIN A FOOTHOLD IN THE U.S.

I'VE ALREADY DONE THE STATES.

NOT REALLY.

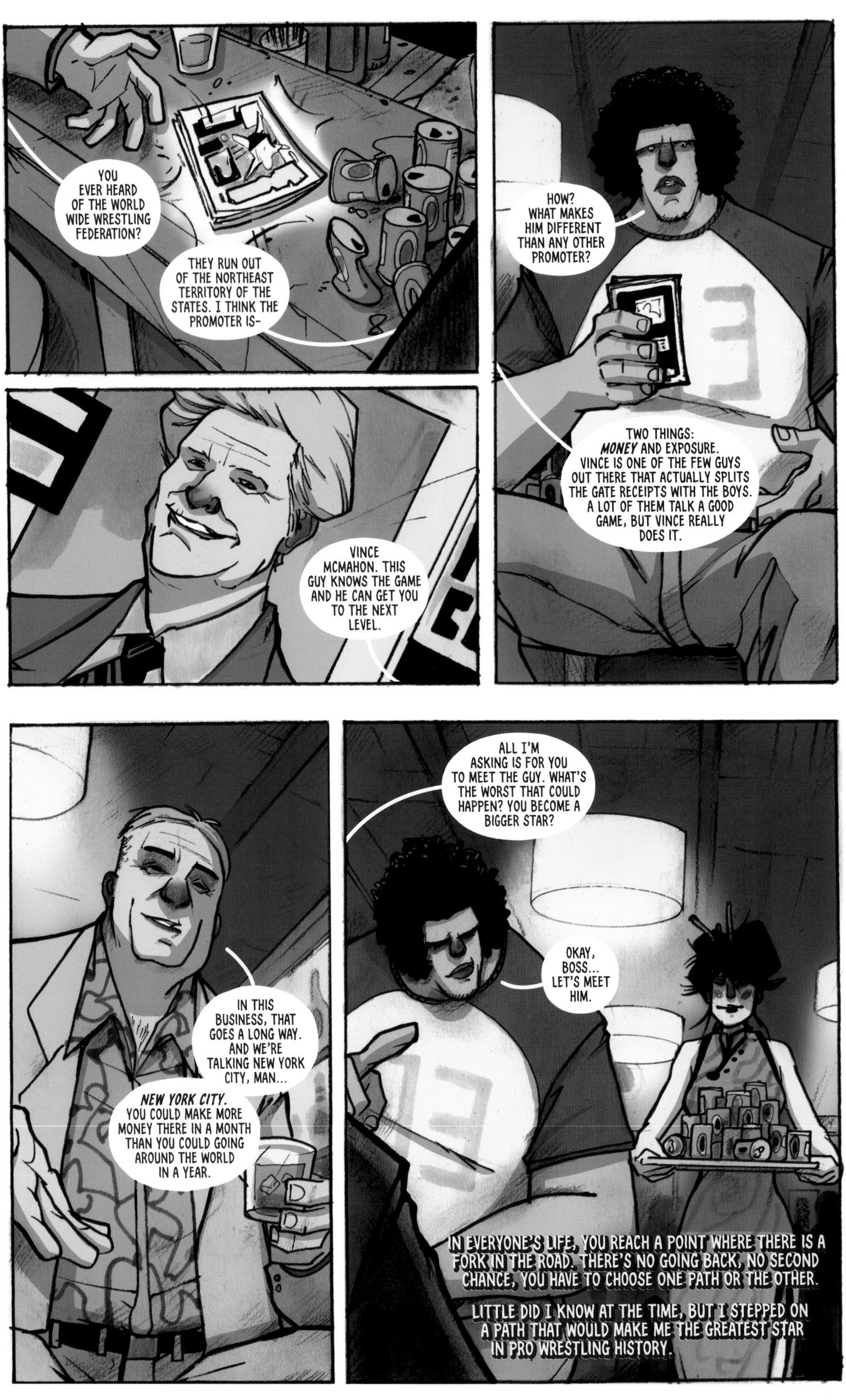
YOU EVER HEARD OF THE WORLD WIDE WRESTLING FEDERATION?
THEY RUN OUT OF THE NORTHEAST TERRITORY OF THE STATES. I THINK THE PROMOTER IS-
HOW? WHAT MAKES HIM DIFFERENT THAN ANY OTHER PROMOTER?
VINCE MCMAHON. THIS GUY KNOWS THE GAME AND HE CAN GET YOU TO THE NEXT LEVEL.
TWO THINGS: *MONEY* AND EXPOSURE. VINCE IS ONE OF THE FEW GUYS OUT THERE THAT ACTUALLY SPLITS THE GATE RECEIPTS WITH THE BOYS. A LOT OF THEM TALK A GOOD GAME, BUT VINCE REALLY DOES IT.
IN THIS BUSINESS, THAT GOES A LONG WAY. AND WE'RE TALKING NEW YORK CITY, MAN...
NEW YORK CITY. YOU COULD MAKE MORE MONEY THERE IN A MONTH THAN YOU COULD GOING AROUND THE WORLD IN A YEAR.
ALL I'M ASKING IS FOR YOU TO MEET THE GUY. WHAT'S THE WORST THAT COULD HAPPEN? YOU BECOME A BIGGER STAR?
OKAY, BOSS... LET'S MEET HIM.
IN EVERYONE'S LIFE, YOU REACH A POINT WHERE THERE IS A FORK IN THE ROAD. THERE'S NO GOING BACK, NO SECOND CHANCE, YOU HAVE TO CHOOSE ONE PATH OR THE OTHER.
LITTLE DID I KNOW AT THE TIME, BUT I STEPPED ON A PATH THAT WOULD MAKE ME THE GREATEST STAR IN PRO WRESTLING HISTORY.

IN THOSE DAYS
THE WRESTLING
SCENE WAS DIVIDED
BY REGIONAL
TERRITORIES.

EVERY AREA
HAD ITS STARS AND
THE SMART PROMOTERS
KNEW NOT TO STEP ON
THE TOES OF THEIR
COLLEAGUES.

I WONDERED
IF I WAS TOO BIG FOR
THOSE TERRITORIES, IF I
WOULD PUSH A PROMOTER TO STEP
ON TOES, OR RATHER, CRUSH THEM?

WELCOME GENTLEMEN. CAN I OFFER YOU ANYTHING?

GOT ANY BEER?

HA! NOT WITH ME.

HE ISN'T KIDDING, VINCE.

I APPRECIATE YOU GUYS MAKING THE TRIP. FRANK, YOU WERE SMART TO REACH OUT TO ME.

YOU COULD ALWAYS TELL WHEN VINCE WAS SERIOUS BECAUSE HE'D PLAY WITH A ROLL OF QUARTERS TO INCREASE HIS CONCENTRATION.

WHATEVER HIS PLANS WERE FOR ME, THEY WERE GOING TO REQUIRE HIS FULL ATTENTION.

ANDRE, WHAT KIND OF CAREER DO YOU WANT?

WHAT DO YOU MEAN, BOSS?

ABOUT SEVEN FEET.

WE'RE GOING TO CHANGE THAT. IMMEDIATELY.

HOW TALL ARE YOU, REALLY?

STAND UP FOR ME... PLEASE.

THE REASON I ASKED YOU ABOUT YOUR CAREER IS BECAUSE I BELIEVE YOU'VE HIT A CEILING. THE AUDIENCE HAS GOTTEN USED TO YOUR INCREDIBLE SIZE AND ATHLETIC PROWESS.

WHAT WE'VE GOT TO DO IS ADD ANOTHER LAYER TO YOUR LEGEND. MAKE YOU BIGGER IN THE EYES OF THE FANS AND THEY'LL FILL IN THE BLANKS OF YOUR MYTHOLOGY.

WHAT DO YOU WANT ME TO DO?

FROM NOW ON, YOU'RE SEVEN-FOOT-FOUR. FIVE-HUNDRED POUNDS. NO MATTER WHAT'S BEEN SAID BEFORE, YOUR ANSWER WILL ALWAYS BE: "SEVEN-FOOT-FOUR, FIVE-HUNDRED POUNDS."

AND... WE'VE GOT TO DO SOMETHING ABOUT YOUR NAME.

VINCE WANTED A NAME THAT ROLLED OFF THE TONGUE. A NAME THAT ANYONE IN ANY COMMUNITY IN ANY TERRITORY COULD UNDERSTAND WITHOUT EXPLANATION.

WORLD WIDE WRESTLING FEDERATION

ANDRE THE GIANT
- VS -
"BEAUTIFUL" BUDDY WOLFE IN HIS DEBUT MATCH

MAIN EVENT

MADISON SQUARE GARDEN
TONITE

"ANDRE THE GIANT" WAS SIMPLE, EFFECTIVE AND CLEAN. A NAME THAT TOLD EVERYONE WHO I WAS WITHOUT A BACKSTORY.

MADISON SQUARE GARDEN.

THE "HOME BASE" OF THE WWWF. EVERYTHING THAT EVER MATTERED IN BOXING AND WRESTLING HAPPENED IN THAT HALLOWED BUILDING.

TOLD YOU THIS WAS A GOOD IDEA.

NEVER DOUBTED YOU FOR A MINUTE, BOSS.

AFTER YOU, MON FRÈRE.

MERCI BEAUCOUP.

MADISON SQUARE GARDEN.

THE PLACE HAD CHARACTER.

THE SMELL OF BURNT OUT CIGARS FROM GRIZZLED SPORTS REPORTERS...

...MIXED WITH CHEAP COLOGNE, FLAT BEERS, AND STALE POPCORN.

TOPPED WITH AN ODOR THAT I COULDN'T IDENTIFY... EITHER IT WAS WEEK-OLD HOT DOG WATER OR SOMETHING TRULY HORRIBLE LEAKING FROM THE BATHROOMS.

I LIKE IT HERE.

VINCE'S PLAN FOR ME WAS SIMPLE, BUT BRILLIANT...

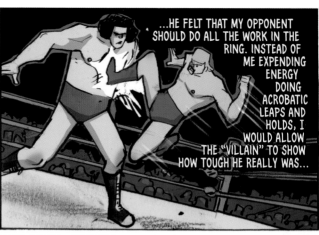

...HE FELT THAT MY OPPONENT SHOULD DO ALL THE WORK IN THE RING. INSTEAD OF ME EXPENDING ENERGY DOING ACROBATIC LEAPS AND HOLDS, I WOULD ALLOW THE "VILLAIN" TO SHOW HOW TOUGH HE REALLY WAS...

...GETTING THE FANS TO BELIEVE THERE WAS A CHANCE FOR ME TO LOSE...

...AND AT THE LAST MOMENT, WHEN ALL SEEMED LOST...

BOOM!!!

THE BIG BOOT!

WHAP!!!

I'D NEVER FORGET THAT NIGHT. IT MUST BE SIMILAR TO GRADUATING FROM HIGH SCHOOL.

VINCE'S FORMULA WOULD PROVE FOOLPROOF FOR THE NEXT TWENTY YEARS.

AND SO IT WENT... I'D TOUCH DOWN IN A TERRITORY, MAKE THEIR HEROES AND VILLAINS LOOK GOOD, AND THEN MOVE ON.

I'D NEVER STAY LONG ENOUGH FOR FANS TO GET TIRED OF ME...

THE OLD SHOWBIZ CLICHÉ OF "LEAVING THEM WANTING MORE" DEFINITELY APPLIED TO ME.

I'D BECOME A SUPERSTAR IN THE PRO WRESTLING WORLD. I'D LEARNED HOW TO PLAY THE GAME FROM THE BEST. BUT...

...I DON'T KNOW IF I WAS HAPPY... SATISFIED, YES, BUT HAPPY... I'M NOT SURE IF I KNEW WHAT THE WORD MEANT.

THERE WAS A PART OF ME THAT UNDERSTOOD THAT I WAS TAKING YEARS OFF MY ALREADY SHORTENED LIFE.

I'D OFTEN SAY A SILENT PRAYER, HOPING FOR A MOMENT OF TRUE HAPPINESS HIDDEN AT THE BOTTOM OF THESE BOTTLES.

LIKE ALL PRAYERS, THERE WAS NO ANSWER.

BEFORE ME, PRO WRESTLERS OCCUPIED A SMALL CORNER OF POP CULTURE. WE WERE CONSIDERED NOTHING MORE THAN GLORIFIED CON-ARTISTS SKILLED IN PULLING SLEIGHT-OF-HAND STUNTS FOR KIDS AND MORONS.

THE LEGEND OF THE "GIANT" SPREAD ACROSS AMERICA LIKE A LIGHTNING BOLT. BEFORE LONG, THE FOLKS SKILLED AT CAPTURING LIGHTNING IN A BOTTLE CAME CALLING FOR ME.

THE SIX MILLION DOLLAR MAN

HEH!

SOMEONE OUT THERE GOT THE BRIGHT IDEA TO DRESS ME UP LIKE A SASQUATCH.

I'D NEVER BEEN ON A REAL "MOVIE" SET BEFORE.

SHOOTING WRESTLING PROMOS IS ONE THING, YET THE SCALE OF ALL THIS WAS BEYOND EVEN ME.

I DID MY BEST TO KEEP MY ANXIETY UNDER WRAPS, BUT I THINK THE PRODUCER COULD SEE MY TERROR FROM A MILE AWAY.

ANDRE! I'M KEN JOHNSON, GREAT TO MEET YOU!

HELLO, MR. JOHNSON.

CALL ME KEN, OR KENNY.

OKAY, BOSS.

GUYS, I WANT YOU TO MEET ANDRE, HE'S GOING TO BE OUR SASQUATCH!

LEE WON'T BE HERE FOR A WHILE, IN THE MEANTIME, I NEED YOU TO GO DOWN TO COSTUME AND MAKEUP SO WE CAN GET YOU READY TO SHOOT TOMORROW.

OKAY, BOSS.

ONE MORE THING, DON'T BE NERVOUS. I KNOW IT'S EASIER SAID THAN DONE, BUT YOU'VE GOT NOTHING TO WORRY ABOUT. IF ANYTHING, LEE AND THE REST OF THE GUYS WERE TERRIFIED OF YOU.

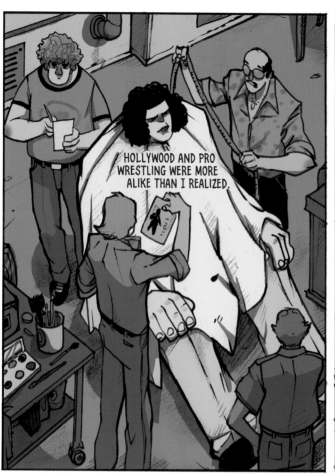

HOLLYWOOD AND PRO WRESTLING WERE MORE ALIKE THAN I REALIZED.

THERE WERE HUNDREDS OF HOURS OF PREP TIME FOR A FINAL PRODUCT THAT LASTED ONLY TWENTY OR THIRTY MINUTES.

EVERYONE INVOLVED WAS PREPARED TO SACRIFICE THEIR BLOOD, SWEAT, AND TEARS FOR THE TEAM. THEIR EFFORTS LARGELY UNAPPRECIATED, BUT SO VERY NECESSARY TO KEEP THE WORLD ENTERTAINED.

PERFECT. YOU'RE PERFECT.

THINK SO, BOSS?

ASK HIM...

HEY THERE, BIG FELLA! NOW, YOU'RE GONNA HAVE TO TAKE IT EASY WITH ME. WE'VE GOT A NICE FIGHT SET UP AND I CAN'T HAVE YOU BREAKING ME IN HALF.

AS SOON AS THE DIRECTOR YELLED "ACTION!" MY NERVOUSNESS WENT AWAY AND I BECAME THE MONSTER THEY WANTED.

THIS WAS INCREDIBLE! I HAD ACHIEVED MORE THAN ANYONE I KNEW. I'D REACHED A WORLD FEW GOT TO SEE, LET ALONE EXPERIENCE.

THEY LOVED MY WORK, SO MUCH I WAS INVITED TO RETURN IN THE FUTURE, IF MY EPISODE MANAGED TO EXCITE THE AUDIENCE.

IT DID!

AN UNFAMILIAR FEELING CLAWED ITS WAY THROUGH MY STOMACH... HAPPINESS.

IT FADED QUICKLY, NOT LONG AFTER THE EPISODE ENDED.

I DIDN'T REALIZE IT BECAUSE I WAS IN THE CENTER OF THE STORM... BUT PRO WRESTLING HAD GONE LEGIT.

I WOULDN'T SAY WE'D BECOME RESPECTABLE...

WRESTLING ARENA

Andre The Giant **VS** Crazy Bull Joe

TONIGHT

...BUT WE'D MOVED OUT OF THE SHADOWY CORNER OF ENTERTAINMENT TO JOIN THE REST OF POP CULTURE IN THE LIMELIGHT.

I'D HAD A HAND IN CREATING A MONSTER. THE FIRST DOMINO FELL AND NO ONE KNEW WHERE IT WOULD LEAD THE BUSINESS.

THE JAPANESE WERE ALWAYS THINKING ABOUT THE FUTURE OF THE SPORT, AND THEY'D TAKEN THE BATON AND RUN WITH IT... AND GIVEN US A FORTUNE WE WERE TOO BLIND TO TAKE SERIOUSLY.

THE BIGGEST JAPANESE STAR OF THE MID-1970S WAS *ANTONIO INOKI.* HIS FEDERATION *SHIN NIHON PURORESU* - OR NEW JAPAN PRO WRESTLING - WAS A JUGGERNAUT OF RATINGS AND AUDIENCE PARTICIPATION.

INOKI WAS A PERFECT COMBINATION OF STRENGTH, SPEED, SKILL, MARTIAL ARTS PROWESS AND SHOWMANSHIP.

LIKE MYSELF, A ONCE-IN-A-LIFETIME TALENT.

I'D ARGUE HIS BEST TALENT WAS MARKETING. HE KNEW HOW TO GET THE FANS INTERESTED IN WHATEVER HE HAD PLANNED FOR *NJPW.*

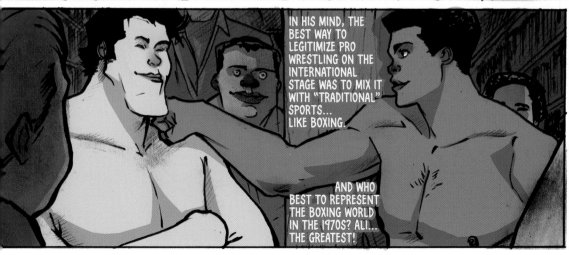

IN HIS MIND, THE BEST WAY TO LEGITIMIZE PRO WRESTLING ON THE INTERNATIONAL STAGE WAS TO MIX IT WITH "TRADITIONAL" SPORTS... LIKE BOXING.

AND WHO BEST TO REPRESENT THE BOXING WORLD IN THE 1970S? ALI... THE GREATEST!

IT WAS CALLED THE "MATCH OF THE CENTURY." I'VE OFTEN WONDERED HOW MANY TIMES YOU CAN SAY THAT BEFORE IT SOUNDS STUPID.

THIS MATCH WAS A DISASTER.

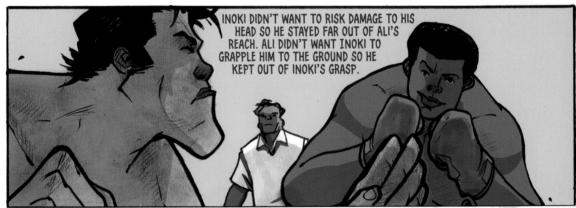

INOKI DIDN'T WANT TO RISK DAMAGE TO HIS HEAD SO HE STAYED FAR OUT OF ALI'S REACH. ALI DIDN'T WANT INOKI TO GRAPPLE HIM TO THE GROUND SO HE KEPT OUT OF INOKI'S GRASP.

IN THE END, INOKI SPENT MOST OF THE MATCH ON THE GROUND, KICKING AT ALI'S LEGS UNTIL THE FINAL BELL RANG.

THE MATCH DID HAVE ITS DESIRED EFFECT. THE ENTIRE WORLD WATCHED IT AND IT BECAME A MASSIVE WINDFALL FOR BOTH MEN, ESPECIALLY INOKI.

WHEN VINCE SAW THE PUBLICITY OF THE INOKI MATCH, THE WHEELS STARTED SPINNING IN HIS HEAD. HE FELT HE SHOULD JOIN THE OTHER PROMOTERS IN BOOKING A SHOW THAT WOULD SERVE AS THE "UNDERCARD" FOR INOKI VS. ALI. HOWEVER, BEFORE THAT HAPPENED, ME AND FRANK HAD TO MAKE A TOUGH DECISION.

ANDRE, FRANK, I'M GLAD YOU'RE HERE. I WANTED TO GIVE YOU BOTH THE ITINERARY FOR THE NEXT SIX MONTHS OF SHOWS.

I'M SENDING YOU TO TEXAS, MISSOURI, CHICAGO, MONTREAL, AND BALTIMORE. ALL THE PROMOTERS HAVE A VARIETY OF OPPONENTS FOR YOU!

THANKS, VINCE.

IF IT'S OKAY WITH YOU, I'D LIKE TO GO BACK TO MY HOTEL AND GET SOME SHUT-EYE.

SURE.

NIGHT, ANDRE.

NIGHT, BOSS.

WHAT'S GOING ON WITH HIM LATELY?

I THINK HE'S TIRED?

OF...?

EVERYTHING. THE TRAVEL. THE WORK. THE BUSINESS. I DON'T THINK HE FINDS JOY IN THIS ANYMORE.

HMN... WE CAN ALWAYS REPLACE HIM. I KNOW YOU VALUE LOYALTY, BUT HE NEEDS TO BE ON BOARD ONE-HUNDRED PERCENT.

YOUR CAREER IS GOING TO GET MORE COMPLICATED. CAN YOU MAKE HIM UNDERSTAND?

"I'LL TRY..."

HOW YOU BEEN, BOSS?

I'M ALL RIGHT.

YOU'RE NOT A GOOD LIAR.

VINCE WANTS YOU TO FIRE ME.

NO. HE WANTS TO KNOW YOU CAN KEEP UP WITH MY CAREER.

"KEEP UP?" ANDRE, I CREATED YOUR CAREER.

YOU THINK I'VE FORGOTTEN?

I'M TIRED, ANDRE. IT HAS NOTHING TO DO WITH YOU, I'M GETTING OLD. SOMEDAY, YOU WILL TOO—

SORRY. I DIDN'T MEAN—

I KNOW YOU DIDN'T.

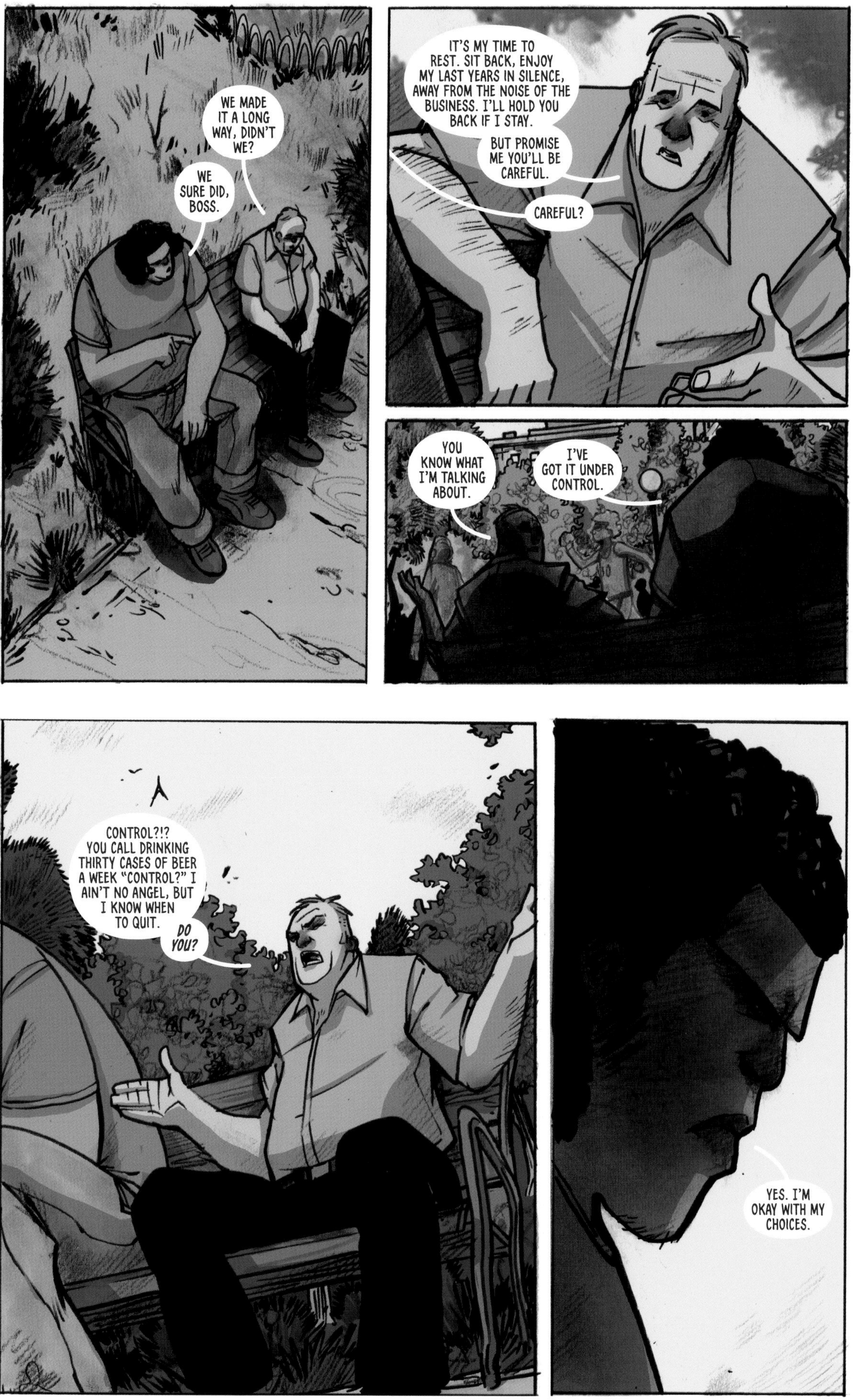
WE MADE IT A LONG WAY, DIDN'T WE?
WE SURE DID, BOSS.
IT'S MY TIME TO REST. SIT BACK, ENJOY MY LAST YEARS IN SILENCE, AWAY FROM THE NOISE OF THE BUSINESS. I'LL HOLD YOU BACK IF I STAY.
BUT PROMISE ME YOU'LL BE CAREFUL.
CAREFUL?
YOU KNOW WHAT I'M TALKING ABOUT.
I'VE GOT IT UNDER CONTROL.
CONTROL?!? YOU CALL DRINKING THIRTY CASES OF BEER A WEEK "CONTROL?" I AIN'T NO ANGEL, BUT I KNOW WHEN TO QUIT.
DO YOU?
YES. I'M OKAY WITH MY CHOICES.

ONE THING. I KNOW YOU CAN TRUST VINCE, BUT KEEP YOUR EYES OPEN. THERE'S A LOT OF FOLKS OUT THERE WHO'D TAKE ADVANTAGE OF YOU THE MINUTE YOUR GUARD GOES DOWN.

MON FRERE...

SO WHAT NEXT, BOSS?

OOOMPH...
I'M GOING TO BOOK A FLIGHT TO SOMEPLACE WARM WHERE THE WOMEN WEAR BIKINIS ALL DAY.

WHEN HE LEFT, IT FELT LIKE THE DOOR HAD BEEN SHUT TO MY PAST.

FRANK HAD BEEN A GUIDING FORCE FOR SO LONG THAT I'D NEVER IMAGINE HE'D BE GONE.

NOW WAS THE TIME TO PUT AWAY CHILDISH THINGS...

ANDRE, THIS IS ARNOLD.

ARNIE, YOU TAKE GOOD CARE OF OUR BOY HERE.

HELLO.

ME AND YOU, WE'RE GONNA DO BIG THINGS!

ARNOLD SKAALAND WAS A TRUSTED CONFIDANTE OF VINCE'S AND HAD A LONG CAREER IN THE WRESTLING BUSINESS, WORKING FOR THE WWWF FOR MANY YEARS.

ARNOLD USED TO BE IN CHARGE OF PRODUCING WRESTLING SHOWS AT THE WESTCHESTER COUNTY CENTER RIGHT OUTSIDE OF NEW YORK CITY.

THAT MAN HAD SEEN MORE MATCHES THAN I'D WRESTLED.

HE KNEW WHAT BUTTONS TO PUSH IN ORDER TO INCREASE YOUR "HEAT" OR CROWD-REACTIONS.

WHAT DO YOU LIKE TO DO FOR FUN?

DRINK AND PLAY CARDS, WHAT ABOUT YOU?

I KNEW YOU TWO WOULD GET ALONG!

WORLD HEAVYWEIGHT TITLE
BACK TO USA

Muhammad Ali
vs.
Chuck Wepner

plus

Ken Norton
vs.
Oscar Bonavena

ANYWAY, GETTING BACK TO THE BOXING VS. WRESTLING IDEA...

...VINCE FOUND THE PERFECT OPPONENT FOR ME: CHUCK WEPNER.

WEPNER WAS YOUR AVERAGE JERSEY CUTTHROAT WHOSE MOUTH MOVED FASTER THAN HIS FISTS.

A FORMER BOUNCER AND U.S. MARINE, WEPNER SHOT TO FAME WHEN HE WAS PICKED OUT OF OBSCURITY TO CHALLENGE ALI IN A SPECIAL MATCH.

THE MATCH WENT THE DISTANCE, WITH WEPNER HOLDING HIS OWN WITH THE CHAMP ALL THE WAY TO THE NINTH ROUND...

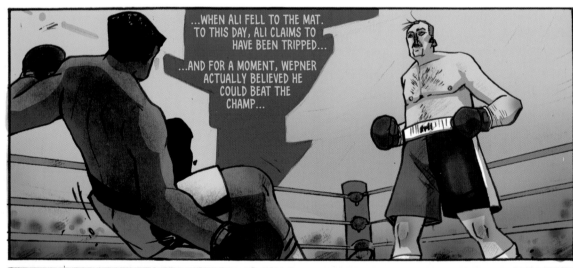

...WHEN ALI FELL TO THE MAT. TO THIS DAY, ALI CLAIMS TO HAVE BEEN TRIPPED...

...AND FOR A MOMENT, WEPNER ACTUALLY BELIEVED HE COULD BEAT THE CHAMP...

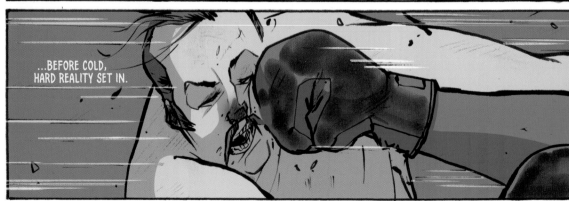

...BEFORE COLD, HARD REALITY SET IN.

THAT'S THE GUY.

YOU SURE, BOSS?

HE'S PERFECT, JUST DUMB ENOUGH TO THINK HE CAN TAKE YOU.

YEARS LATER, IT WAS RUMORED THAT WEPNER'S FIGHT WITH ALI WAS SYLVESTER STALLONE'S INSPIRATION FOR THE ROCKY BALBOA CHARACTER, DEPENDING ON WHO YOU BELIEVED.

JUNE 25 1975

ON THE NIGHT OF INOKI VS. ALI

WE BOTH HAD TO BE CAREFUL NOT TO KILL THE OTHER GUY. IT WAS SET UP TO MAXIMIZE OUR EXPOSURE TO THE NATIONAL AUDIENCE.

OF COURSE, THINGS GOT A LITTLE OUT OF HAND.

AFTER DANCING AROUND THE RING FOR THREE ROUNDS, WEPNER DECIDES TO TOSS A HARD ONE.

WHAP!

I COULD TAKE IT, BUT HE HAD TO KNOW, ALL THE FIGHTERS HAD TO KNOW THAT YOU DON'T GET TO SUCKER PUNCH THE "EIGHTH WONDER OF THE WORLD."

I THINK HE GOT THE MESSAGE.

IT WASN'T A MASTERPIECE, BUT IT GOT PEOPLE TALKING. AND THAT'S WHAT VINCE WANTED ALL ALONG.

AND I'D SETTLED THE "BOXING VS. WRESTLER" DEBATE ONCE AND FOR ALL. INOKI AND ALI NEVER COULD FINISH THAT STORY.

SON, THE WORLD IS YOURS!

THE MOST DANGEROUS COMBINATION ON EARTH IS YOUTH, EGO, AND VALIDATION. SEPARATELY, THEY WERE PROBLEMATIC, TOGETHER, IT WAS AN ATOMIC BOMB OF HUMAN STUPIDITY.

IF I'D EVER KNOWN THE MEANING OF "MODERATION" I'D CERTAINLY FORGOTTEN IT BY NOW. EXCESS WAS ENTRENCHED AS MY STATUS QUO.

THERE WAS A TIME WHEN I'D HAVE IGNORED THEM...

I REALLY TRIED...

HE AIN'T SO TOUGH.

JUST A FAT BAG OF GAS.

I HEARD HE LIKES LITTLE GIRLS.

YOU MEAN LITTLE BOYS?

HAH!

I FOUND A PAIR OF LOADED DIAPERS IN THE TRASH CAN. LOOKED LIKE THEY COULD FIT AROUND THE ASS OF A HIPPO!

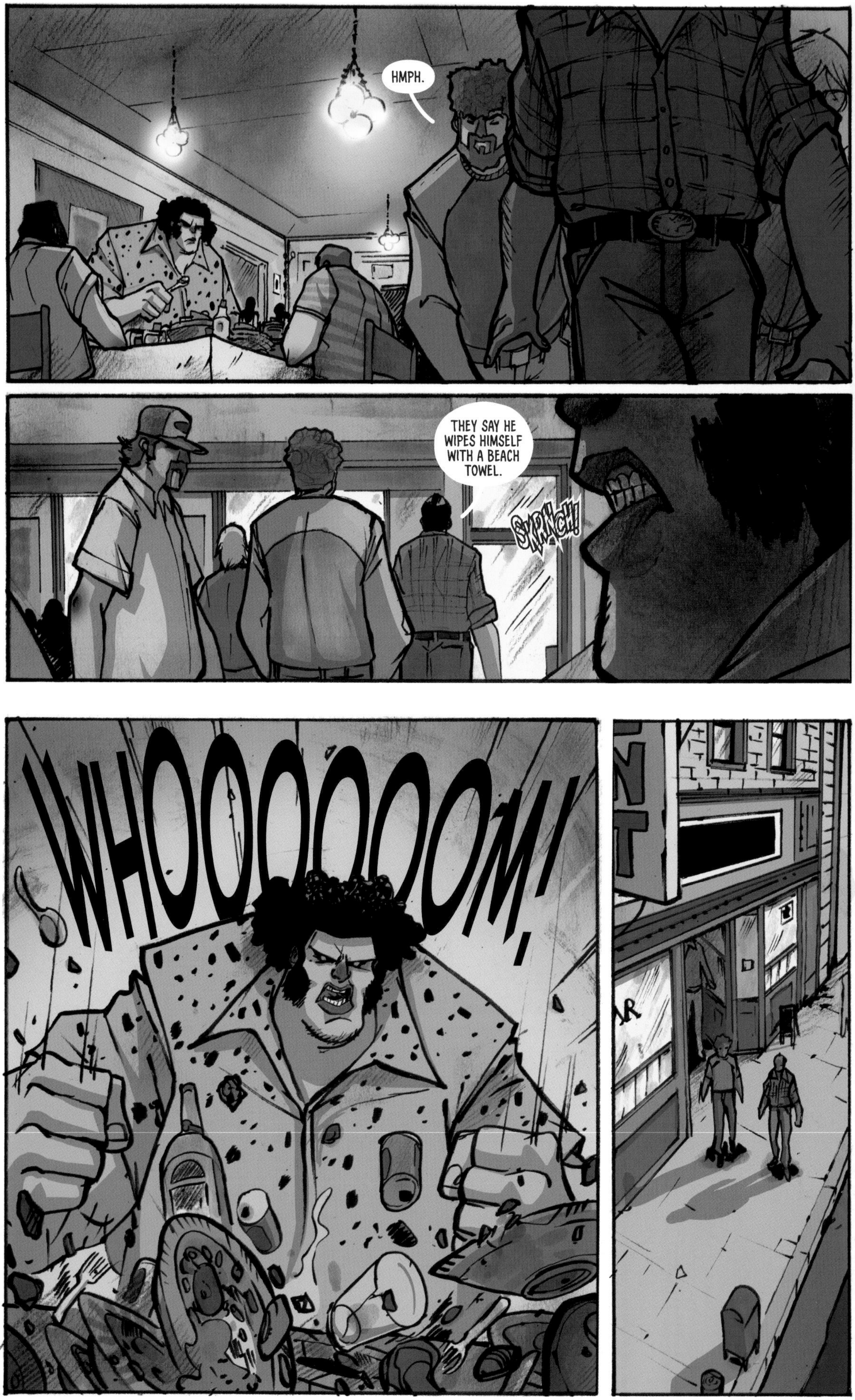
HMPH.
THEY SAY HE WIPES HIMSELF WITH A BEACH TOWEL.
SKRNCH!
WHOOOOOOM!

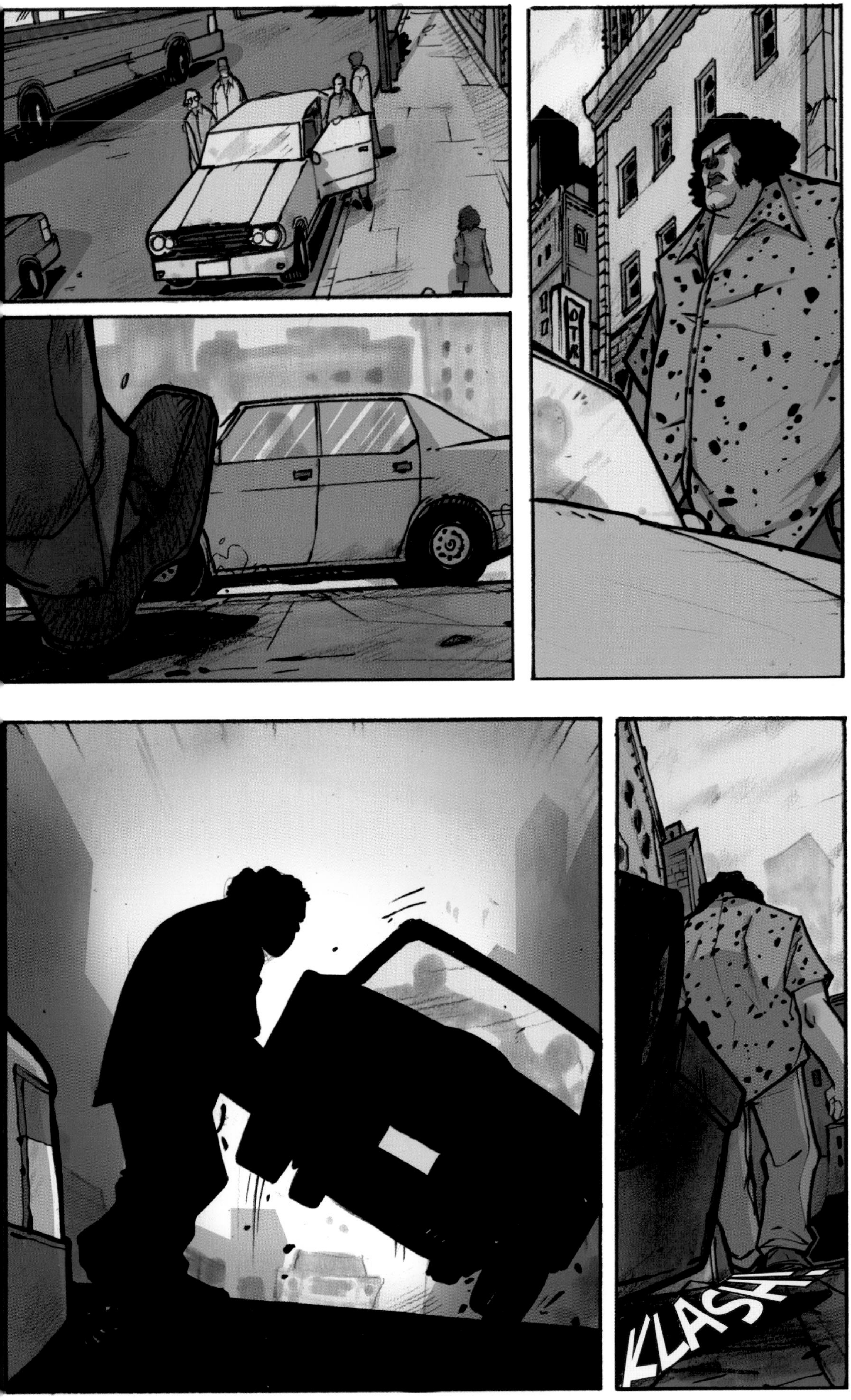
KLASH!

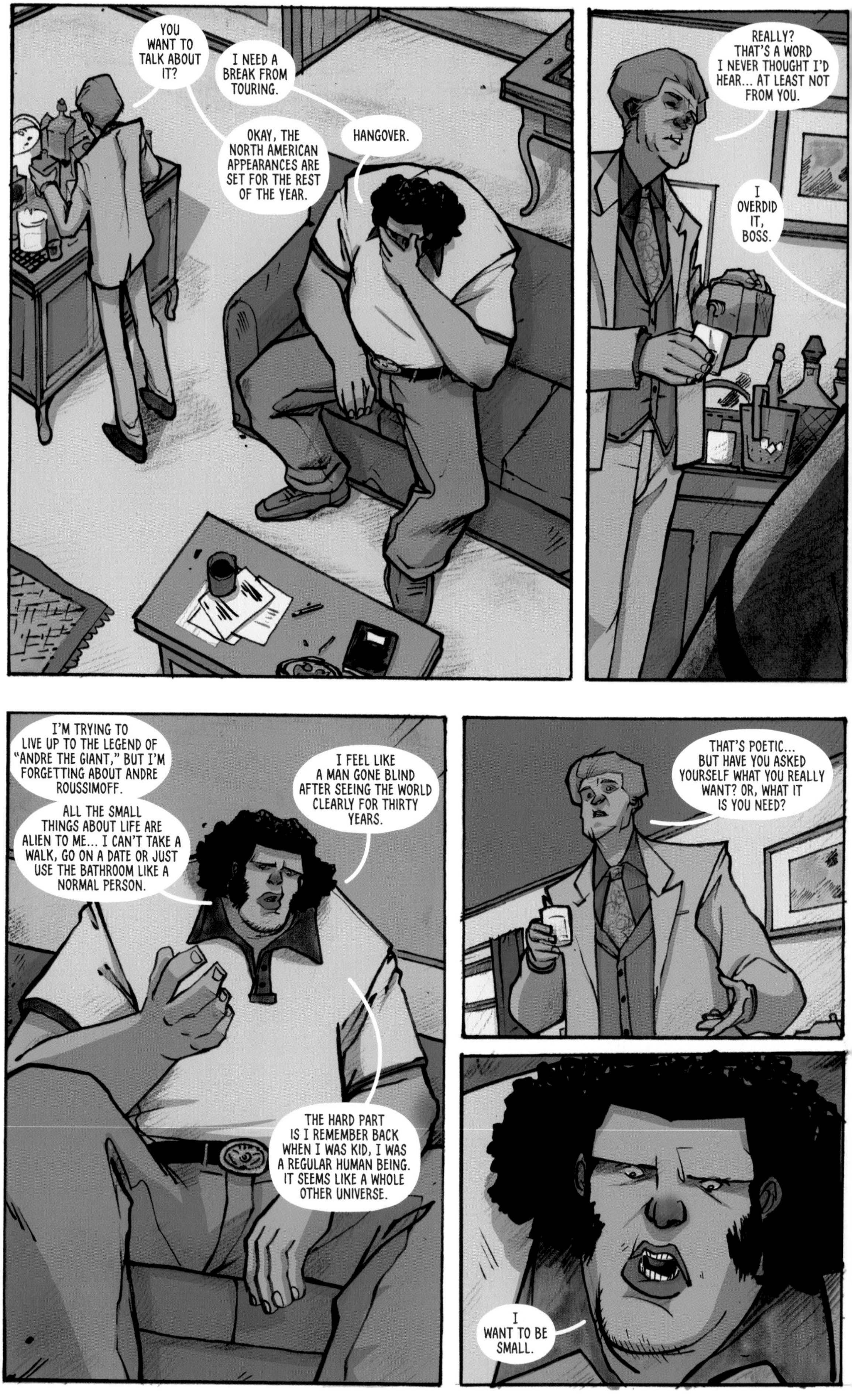
YOU WANT TO TALK ABOUT IT?
I NEED A BREAK FROM TOURING.
OKAY, THE NORTH AMERICAN APPEARANCES ARE SET FOR THE REST OF THE YEAR.
HANGOVER.
REALLY? THAT'S A WORD I NEVER THOUGHT I'D HEAR... AT LEAST NOT FROM YOU.
I OVERDID IT, BOSS.
I'M TRYING TO LIVE UP TO THE LEGEND OF "ANDRE THE GIANT," BUT I'M FORGETTING ABOUT ANDRE ROUSSIMOFF.
ALL THE SMALL THINGS ABOUT LIFE ARE ALIEN TO ME... I CAN'T TAKE A WALK, GO ON A DATE OR JUST USE THE BATHROOM LIKE A NORMAL PERSON.
I FEEL LIKE A MAN GONE BLIND AFTER SEEING THE WORLD CLEARLY FOR THIRTY YEARS.
THE HARD PART IS I REMEMBER BACK WHEN I WAS KID, I WAS A REGULAR HUMAN BEING. IT SEEMS LIKE A WHOLE OTHER UNIVERSE.
THAT'S POETIC... BUT HAVE YOU ASKED YOURSELF WHAT YOU REALLY WANT? OR, WHAT IT IS YOU NEED?
I WANT TO BE SMALL.

I DECIDED TO GO BACK TO JAPAN FOR A LITTLE WHILE. THERE WAS A CERTAIN LOGIC, A CLARITY WITH THE JAPANESE PEOPLE THAT I COULDN'T FIND ANYPLACE ELSE.

I'LL HANDLE THIS...

SIR, A PLEASURE TO HAVE YOU CHOOSE OUR AIRLINE AGAIN. WHAT SEEMS TO BE THE PROBLEM?

NO ROOM.

WHAT DO YOU MEAN YOU CAN'T ACCOMMODATE ME? I'VE FLOWN TO JAPAN MANY TIMES!

YOU'VE USUALLY B-BOOKED W-WELL IN ADVANCE AND PURCHASED MULTIPLE SEATS. THERE... JUST ISN'T ENOUGH ROOM FOR YOU, SIR.

THERE IS AN OPTION, IF YOU'LL BE SO KIND TO CONSIDER IT. WE CAN HAVE YOU SIT ON THE FLOOR NEAR OUR GALLEY. IT'S NOT THE BEST EXPERIENCE, BUT YOU'LL HAVE THE SPACE YOU NEED AND FULL ACCESS TO THE MINI-BAR.

FOR TWELVE HOURS...?

WITH MINI-BAR ACCESS.

THEY HAD ME AT MINI-BAR.

THE DRINKING AND PARTYING WAS GETTING OUT OF HAND... ...AND THINGS GOT DOWNRIGHT UGLY DURING A TOUR OF JAPAN.

...BUT THE TRUE LEADER OF THIS GROUP WAS A WRESTLER BY THE NAME OF *BAD NEWS ALLEN*.

I LOVED THE ATTENTION FROM THE BOYS. THEY LOOKED UP TO ME, THEY WANTED ME TO LIKE THEM, AND I FELT LIKE THEIR LEADER...

ALLEN WAS CONSIDERED A TOUGH-GUY... NOT PHONY, BOASTFUL TOUGH... BUT RIP-YOUR-JAW-OUT-OF-YOUR-FACE TOUGH.

HE WAS A WORLD-CHAMPION IN JUDO, WINNING GOLD AT THE PAN-AMERICAN GAMES AND THE BRONZE AT THE 1976 OLYMPICS.

NOT A MAN TO BE TRIFLED WITH...

SO THE !!*$#@¢ SAID: "*WHY ELSE* WOULD I HAVE THESE BOOKS!?!"

IN MY HAZE OF ARROGANCE AND STUPIDITY, I DIDN'T CARE.

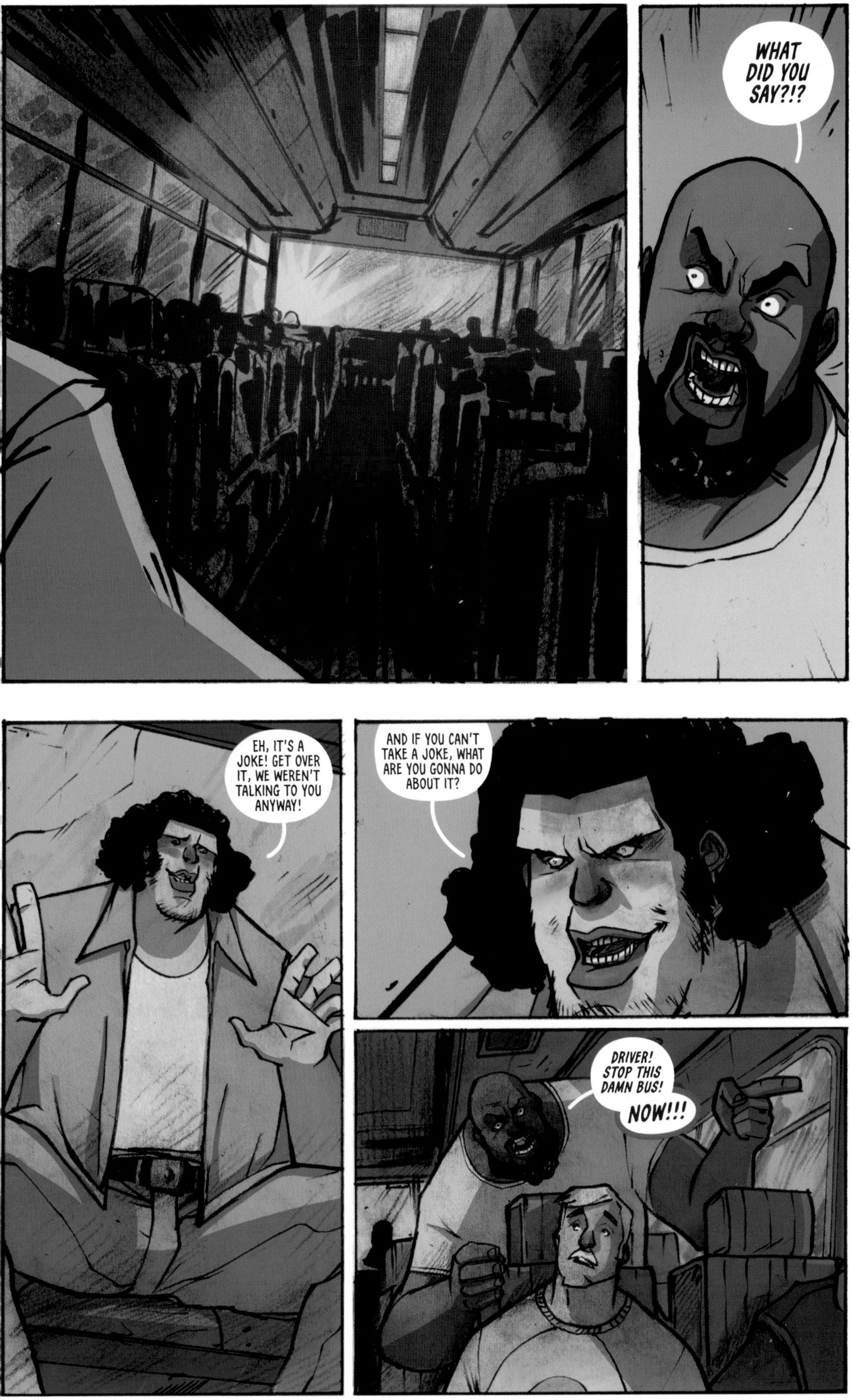
WHAT DID YOU SAY?!?
EH, IT'S A JOKE! GET OVER IT, WE WEREN'T TALKING TO YOU ANYWAY!
AND IF YOU CAN'T TAKE A JOKE, WHAT ARE YOU GONNA DO ABOUT IT?
DRIVER! STOP THIS DAMN BUS!
NOW!!!

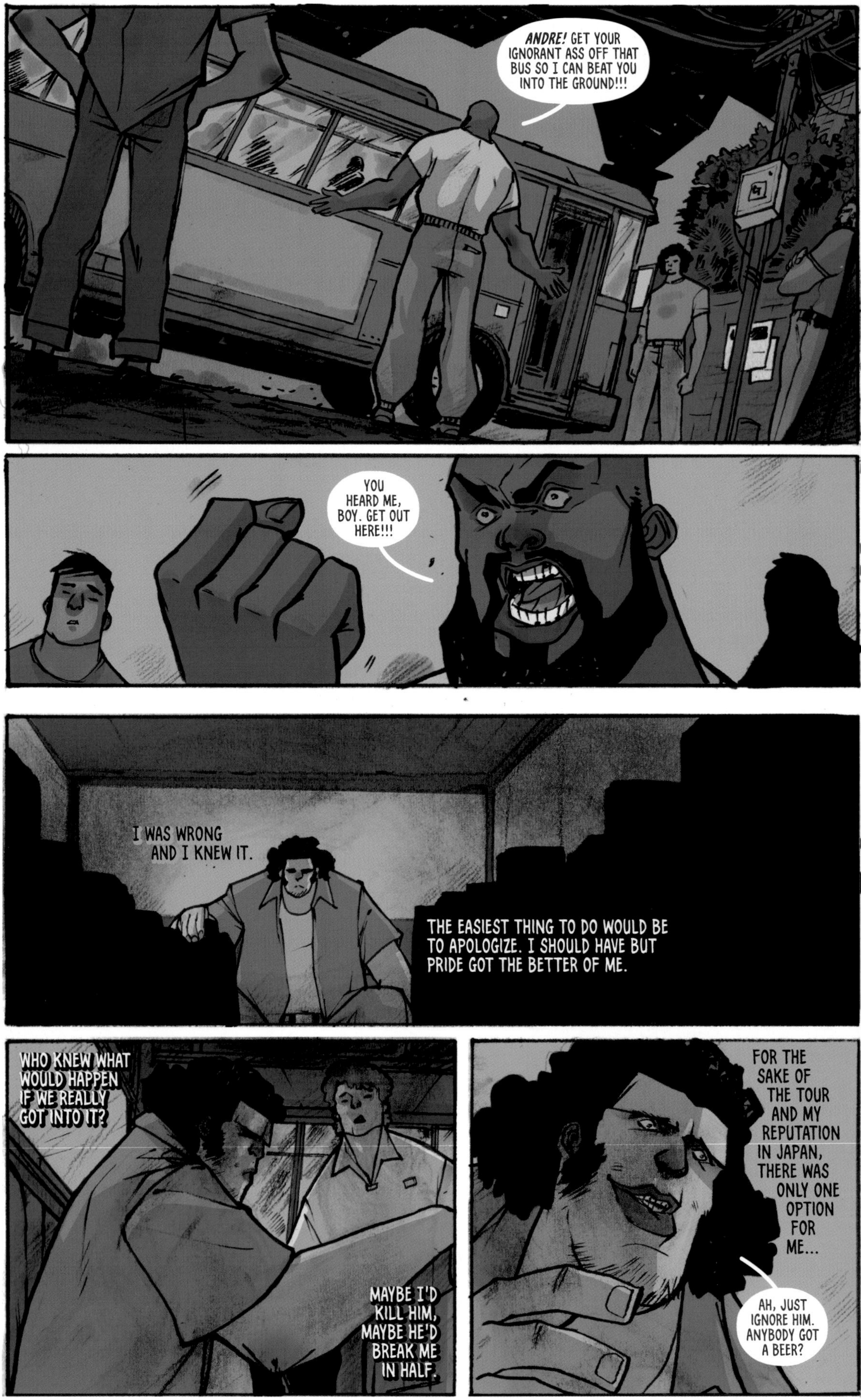
ANDRE! GET YOUR IGNORANT ASS OFF THAT BUS SO I CAN BEAT YOU INTO THE GROUND!!!
YOU HEARD ME, BOY. GET OUT HERE!!!
I WAS WRONG AND I KNEW IT.
THE EASIEST THING TO DO WOULD BE TO APOLOGIZE. I SHOULD HAVE BUT PRIDE GOT THE BETTER OF ME.
WHO KNEW WHAT WOULD HAPPEN IF WE REALLY GOT INTO IT?
MAYBE I'D KILL HIM, MAYBE HE'D BREAK ME IN HALF.
FOR THE SAKE OF THE TOUR AND MY REPUTATION IN JAPAN, THERE WAS ONLY ONE OPTION FOR ME...
AH, JUST IGNORE HIM. ANYBODY GOT A BEER?

MY PRIDE WOULDN'T ALLOW ME TO APOLOGIZE TO HIM AT FIRST. I KNEW HE'D COME TO ME. ALLEN WAS A STAND-UP GUY.

WHAT THE HELL IS THE MATTER WITH YOU?

IT WAS A JOKE. I DIDN'T MEAN—

YOU SURPRISED ME, MAN. I DIDN'T EXPECT TO HEAR THAT CRAP FROM YOU!

I DON'T CARE WHERE YOU'RE FROM, YOU AIN'T GOT THE RIGHT TO DISRESPECT ME.

WE'VE GOT ANOTHER WEEK OR SO ON THIS TOUR. I DON'T WANT TO HEAR ANY MORE OF THIS NONSENSE.

YOU GOT IT?

YEA.

THERE WAS NOTHING ELSE TO BE SAID.

I DID LEARN A FEW THINGS DURING THAT TOUR....

...THE FIRST THING WAS THAT I HAD BECOME A MONSTER WITHOUT REALIZING IT.

THE EXCESSES OF MY LIFE HAD PUSHED ME INTO AN UNFAMILIAR PLACE. I WASN'T RAISED TO BE A DISRESPECTFUL LOUT. BUT THAT'S HOW SOME PEOPLE SAW ME...

KRRRRASSSHHHHH!!!

...THE OTHER THING I LEARNED?

I STILL HAD A LOT OF GROWING UP TO DO.

I NEEDED SOMETHING STABLE. THE LIFE OF A WRESTLER IS NOT A CHARMED ONE. YOU LIVE OFF OF THE ADRENALINE... YOU LIVE OFF OF THE ROAR OF THE CROWD... THAT POP WHEN YOU STEP INTO THE ARENA...

...IT ALL LED TO GROUPIES, HUNDREDS OF WILLING LADIES EAGER TO SHOW THEIR APPRECIATION FOR YOU.

I COULD REMEMBER NONE OF THEM.

WELL... THAT'S NOT TRUE... THERE WAS A WOMAN I DATED FOR SEVEN YEARS. IF YOU COULD CALL IT "DATING." HER NAME WAS JEAN.

SHE WRESTLED UNDER THE NAME "TRIXIE COLT" AND WAS AN INTEGRAL PART OF THE SCENE. UNFORTUNATELY, I LET EVERYONE BELIEVE SHE WAS A RING RAT – A COMMON GROUPIE I ENTERTAINED WHENEVER IN THE MOOD.

SHE BECAME PREGNANT AND HAD MY DAUGHTER ROBIN. A MIRACLE REALLY... I WAS TOLD I'D BE STERILE. BECAUSE OF THIS I BELIEVED SHE WAS A LIAR.

Dad... should I call you that? Biologically you're my father, but I've only seen you twice over the last ten years. I'm not writing this letter to blame you for anything. I just want you to know how I feel...

....I understand you believed my mother was lying. You had been told that you couldn't get a woman pregnant. But even after the bloodtest when I was two years old, you still weren't there for me.

In that North Carolina courtroom, it took the weight of the law to get you to finally understand who I was. Years of listening to the wrong people who kept my mother away from you did irreparable damage.

I wished I could have known what it was like to have a dad in my life. I'd take a mailman or carpenter over a global superstar whose shadow hung over our lives.

I know you wanted me to join you on your farm... but I wouldn't come without my mother. I wouldn't go anywhere without mom. I got the impression it hurt you deeply...

...maybe there was a tiny part of me that wanted to hurt you, to make you feel the loss and pain I dealt with every day.

Like I said, I'm not trying to blame you for anything. Nobody was the good guy. We're all responsible for how this turned out.

It's hell... what we need we can't have because it's impossible to reverse time and make better decisions... to have the courage it takes to reach out...

...when we do reach out, all those wrestlers mom thought were her friends have put up a wall around you. They shut us out. Permanently.

I truly hope this letter finds you in good health. Maybe one day we can sit down and just talk. I'd like to know more about you... and I could tell you about my life, my school, my friends... all the little things dads should know.

Until then... best regards.

- Your daughter Robin.

THE WRESTLING WORLD WAS CHANGING FASTER THAN ANY OF US COULD HANDLE. THERE WERE NEW STARS BEING BORN.

ONE OF THEM, A KID THEY CALLED "TERRY BOULDER" AND "STERLING GOLDEN" WOULD EVENTUALLY BE KNOWN TO THE ENTIRE PLANET AS *HULK HOGAN*.

VINCE HAD SUGGESTED THAT WE WORK TOGETHER BECAUSE THE AUDIENCE WOULD BELIEVE HE'D HAVE A LEGIT CHANCE TO TAKE ME DOWN.

I RESPECTED VINCE'S WISHES, BUT I DIDN'T LIKE HOGAN... NOT AT FIRST.

HOGAN'S REPUTATION AS AN ARROGANT SHOWBOAT PRECEDED HIM.

HE HAD BEEN SO PRIDEFUL THAT HIS TRAINER - HIRO MATSUDA - BROKE HIS LEG IN ORDER TO TEACH HIM SOME RESPECT.

THE WORD GOING AROUND WAS THAT HOGAN WAS LAZY AND COASTED ON HIS IMPRESSIVE PHYSIQUE AND GOOD LOOKS TO CARRY HIM OVER THE TOP.

I DESPISED PRIMA DONNAS - ALL THE GUYS I'D WORKED WITH WERE SERIOUS ABOUT THE CRAFT.

I WANTED TO SHOW HIM HOW SERIOUS I WAS...

WHAP!!!

THOK!

...I THINK HE GOT THE MESSAGE.

TO HIS CREDIT, HE NEVER WHINED, COMPLAINED OR RAN TO THE BOSSES...

...I HAD TO RESPECT HIS TOUGHNESS, EVEN THOUGH I BEAT THE KID TO WITHIN AN INCH OF HIS LIFE.

IF THERE WAS ONE THING VINCE KNEW HOW TO DO, IT WAS RECOGNIZE A STAR EARLY IN THEIR CAREER.

HOGAN HAD ALL THE QUALITIES OF A WRESTLING SUPERSTAR: GOOD LOOKS, SIZE, A PERFECT PHYSIQUE...

...AND THAT ONE ELUSIVE THING THAT CANNOT BE TAUGHT, LEARNED OR PURCHASED...

CHARISMA.

WE'D HAD A SERIES OF BATTLES ACROSS THE NORTHEAST THAT ONLY INTENSIFIED OUR FEUD. THERE HAD BEEN NO CLEAR VICTOR.

THE WAR CULMINATED AT THE "SHOWDOWN AT SHEA."

AUGUST 9 1980

THROUGHOUT MY CAREER, I'D BEEN VERY CAREFUL OF WHO I'D LET GET THE UPPER HAND.

I'D BEEN SLAMMED A FEW TIMES IN JAPAN, BUT THE OLD ADAGE WAS: "IF IT DIDN'T HAPPEN ON TV, IN AMERICA, THEN IT DIDN'T HAPPEN." THE WWF HAD AN INTERESTING WAY OF DEALING WITH PRO WRESTLING HISTORY.

I'D PICKED UP HOGAN TO FINISH HIM OFF WITH A BODY SLAM....

...BUT HIS LEGS POPPED THE REF ON HIS NOGGIN.

WITH THE REF DOWN, HOGAN HAD THE OPPORTUNITY TO BLINDSIDE ME.

WHOOOOOM!

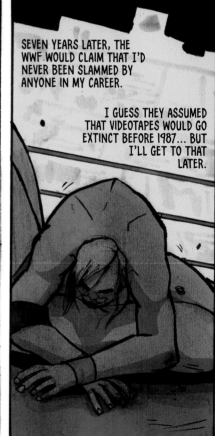

SEVEN YEARS LATER, THE WWF WOULD CLAIM THAT I'D NEVER BEEN SLAMMED BY ANYONE IN MY CAREER.

I GUESS THEY ASSUMED THAT VIDEOTAPES WOULD GO EXTINCT BEFORE 1987... BUT I'LL GET TO THAT LATER.

WHAP!!!

1-
2-
3!!!

HOGAN HAD KICKED OUT OF THE PINFALL AT THE TWO-COUNT, BUT THE REF DIDN'T SEE IT.

THIS SET UP A MOMENT THAT WOULD CATAPULT HOGAN'S CAREER INTO THE *STRATOSPHERE*.

THUD!!!

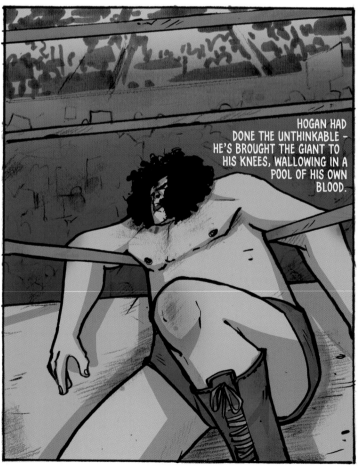

HOGAN HAD DONE THE UNTHINKABLE — HE'S BROUGHT THE GIANT TO HIS KNEES, WALLOWING IN A POOL OF HIS OWN BLOOD.

WE'D CREATED A NEW LEGEND IN HOGAN. BY "WE" I MEANT MYSELF, HOGAN... AND VINCE MCMAHON JR.

VINCE HAD A SON ALSO NAMED VINCE. BUT JUNIOR DIDN'T MEET HIS FATHER UNTIL HE WAS A TEENAGER AND THEIR RELATIONSHIP WAS SOMEWHAT STRAINED. JUNIOR WANTED TO BE INVOLVED IN ALL ASPECTS OF THE WRESTLING BIZ, INCLUDING PERFORMING. BUT SENIOR SCOLDED HIM, MAKING SURE HE UNDERSTOOD THE ROLE OF THE PROMOTER IS TO STAY *BEHIND* THE SCENES.

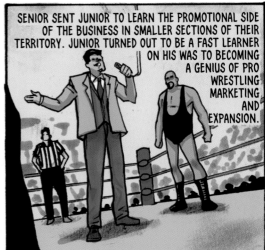

SENIOR SENT JUNIOR TO LEARN THE PROMOTIONAL SIDE OF THE BUSINESS IN SMALLER SECTIONS OF THEIR TERRITORY. JUNIOR TURNED OUT TO BE A FAST LEARNER ON HIS WAS TO BECOMING A GENIUS OF PRO WRESTLING MARKETING AND EXPANSION.

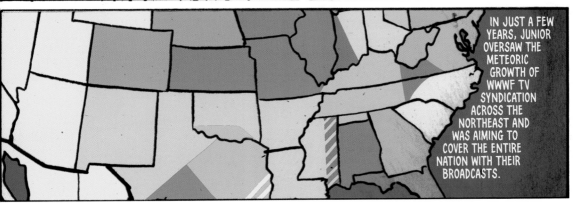

IN JUST A FEW YEARS, JUNIOR OVERSAW THE METEORIC GROWTH OF WWWF TV SYNDICATION ACROSS THE NORTHEAST AND WAS AIMING TO COVER THE ENTIRE NATION WITH THEIR BROADCASTS.

I GOT ALONG FINE WITH JUNIOR. AS LONG AS HIS FATHER WAS THERE TO TEMPER JUNIOR'S AMBITIONS THE COMPANY WAS STABLE AND THE BOYS WERE HAPPY.

IN TIME, SENIOR'S HEALTH WOULD FADE AND JUNIOR WOULD ACQUIRE THE RIGHTS TO CAPITOL WRESTLING CO., LOCK, STOCK AND BARREL. THE WRESTLING BIZ WOULD NEVER BE THE SAME AGAIN.

BUT I'M GETTING AHEAD OF MYSELF...

THE DAY CAME WHEN I BROKE MY ANKLE.

AT THAT TIME I WAS IN THE MIDST OF A BITTER FEUD WITH A POWERFUL WRESTLER BY THE NAME OF *KILLER KHAN*.

HE WAS A GOOD GUY, A JAPANESE WRESTLER PRETENDING TO BE A WILD MONGOLIAN ASSASSIN.

I DON'T KNOW HOW I DID IT, BUT I PLANTED MY FOOT THE WRONG WAY, AND SNAP, CRACKLE, POP!

SNAP!

KRACK!!!

IN THE WRESTLING WORLD, A REAL-LIFE INJURY NOT SUSTAINED IN THE RING HAS TO BE EXPLAINED IN FRONT OF THE AUDIENCE. IF FANS BELIEVED THAT KHAN PUT ME IN THE HOSPITAL, THE EVENTUAL "REVENGE" MATCH WOULD SELL AN EXTRA THOUSAND TICKETS.

IN THE MEANTIME, I HAD TO WAIT FOR A SPECIALLY-CONSTRUCTED HOSPITAL BED AND DEAL WITH THE FACT THAT THERE WASN'T A PAIR OF CRUTCHES ON EARTH THAT COULD SUPPORT MY FRAME.

THE REHAB PROCESS WAS LONG, SLOW AND PAINFUL. THERE WAS NOTHING I COULD DO EXCEPT LET THE HEALING TAKE PLACE.

BY 1983, MY DISEASE FINALLY CAUGHT UP WITH ME. MY BODY COULD NO LONGER GROW, SO THERE WERE CHANGES IN MY PHYSIQUE AND FACE.

IT FELT LIKE I AGED FIVE MONTHS PER WEEK. AT THIS RATE, I'D BE DEAD IN A COUPLE OF YEARS.

I MENTIONED THAT VINCE JUNIOR HAD TAKEN OVER HIS FATHER'S COMPANY. THE DEAL WAS FINALIZED IN '83 AND JUNIOR IMMEDIATELY BEGAN TO CHANGE HOW THINGS WERE DONE.

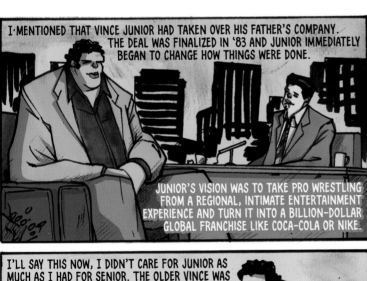

JUNIOR'S VISION WAS TO TAKE PRO WRESTLING FROM A REGIONAL, INTIMATE ENTERTAINMENT EXPERIENCE AND TURN IT INTO A BILLION-DOLLAR GLOBAL FRANCHISE LIKE COCA-COLA OR NIKE.

I'LL SAY THIS NOW, I DIDN'T CARE FOR JUNIOR AS MUCH AS I HAD FOR SENIOR. THE OLDER VINCE WAS A MAN OF HIS WORD. IN ALL THE TIME I WORKED FOR SENIOR, I'D NEVER HAD TO SIGN A CONTRACT, OUR HANDSHAKE AGREEMENT WAS ENOUGH.

WITH VINCE JUNIOR... WELL, BEFORE YOU SIGNED ANYTHING HE GAVE YOU, IT WAS A GOOD IDEA TO RUN IT PAST TEN LAWYERS FIRST (BERNIE SPIEGEL).

VINCE McMAHON

AND IF YOU'RE WONDERING HOW JUNIOR COULD TAKE A REGIONAL PRO WRESTLING COMPANY AND TURN IT INTO THE LARGEST SPORTS ENTERTAINMENT COMPANY IN THE WORLD IN A MATTER OF YEARS, I'LL EXPLAIN...

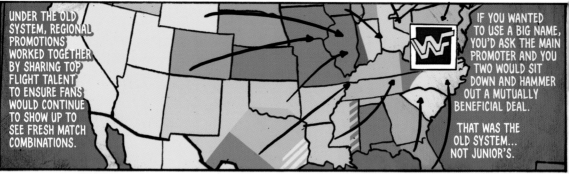

UNDER THE OLD SYSTEM, REGIONAL PROMOTIONS WORKED TOGETHER BY SHARING TOP FLIGHT TALENT TO ENSURE FANS WOULD CONTINUE TO SHOW UP TO SEE FRESH MATCH COMBINATIONS.

IF YOU WANTED TO USE A BIG NAME, YOU'D ASK THE MAIN PROMOTER AND YOU TWO WOULD SIT DOWN AND HAMMER OUT A MUTUALLY BENEFICIAL DEAL.

THAT WAS THE OLD SYSTEM... NOT JUNIOR'S.

JUNIOR BROKE THE CODE... HE POACHED GUYS FROM ALL OVER....

FROM THE MID-ATLANTIC REGION HE GRABBED RICKY STEAMBOAT, RODDY PIPER, GREG VALENTINE, BOB ORTON...

FROM BILL WATTS' MID-SOUTH PROMOTION HE GRABBED THE JUNKYARD DOG....

JUNIOR MERCILESSLY GUTTED VERNE GAGNE'S AWA PROMOTION SO THOROUGHLY THAT THEY NEVER TRULY RECOVERED FROM THE LOSS OF THESE IRREPLACEABLE TALENTS.

IN ONE FELL SWOOP, JUNIOR MANAGED TO BUILD A ROSTER OF LEGENDS WHILE SIGNIFICANTLY WEAKENING A FEW OF HIS TERRITORIAL RIVALS.

IN HOGAN, JUNIOR GOT THE ALL-AMERICAN SUPERHERO THAT HE NEEDED TO BE THE PUBLIC FACE OF HIS COMPANY.

I REALIZED THAT WHILE I WAS STILL AN "ATTRACTION" I WAS NO LONGER "THE MAN." IT WAS HOGAN'S TURN TO RUN WITH THE BALL. HE WAS MORE THAN CAPABLE. ALL THAT REMAINED WAS FINDING A VEHICLE TO GET HIS PRODUCT TO THE MASSES.

THE ROCK 'N WRESTLING CONNECTION WAS A BRILLIANT MOVE BY JUNIOR. MUSIC TELEVISION WAS HITTING THE SCENE AT THE SAME TIME AND PRO WRESTLING BECAME A STRANGE BEDFELLOW.

FOR MANY YOUNG PEOPLE, PRO WRESTLING BECAME A "COOL" THING, NO LONGER RESERVED FOR HILLBILLIES AND DOCKWORKERS.

ANDRE! GOOD TO SEE YOU! I WANTED TO TALK ABOUT YOUR ROLE IN MY SPECIAL PROJECT.

SPECIAL PROJECT?

HA, I HAVEN'T TOLD YOU ABOUT IT YET? SORRY, I'VE BEEN BUSY AND YOU'VE BEEN MAKING MOVIES... WHAT WAS IT – "MICKEY AND MAUDE" AND THAT "CONAN" SEQUEL?

NEXT YEAR I WANT TO DO SOMETHING BIG! REAL BIG. IF IT DOESN'T WORK, IT COULD SINK THE COMPANY AND NONE OF US WANT THAT.

RIGHT, BOSS.

I WANT TO KNOW THAT I CAN COUNT ON YOUR INVOLVEMENT?

OF COURSE, IS THERE ANY DOUBT?

WITH ALL THE CHANGES AROUND HERE, I WASN'T SURE WHAT YOU NEEDED ME TO DO.

ANDRE, I KNOW YOU HAVEN'T BEEN HAPPY WITH THE DIRECTION I'VE TAKEN THE COMPANY. MY FATHER HAD A SPECIAL CONNECTION WITH YOU THAT WE DON'T SHARE.

BUT UNDERSTAND THIS, YOU MEAN A LOT TO ME, AND MORE IMPORTANT, YOU MEAN A LOT TO THE MCMAHON FAMILY.

YOU'LL ALWAYS HAVE A HOME HERE.

THAT'S GOOD TO HEAR.

SO THIS REPRESENTS THE FUTURE OF PROFESSIONAL WRESTLING... SPORTS ENTERTAINMENT... IN THE UNITED STATES!

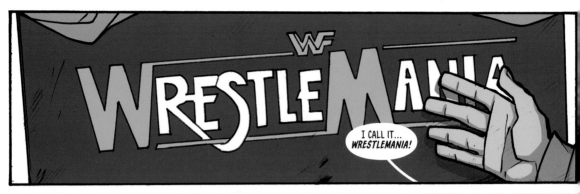

I CALL IT... WRESTLEMANIA!

MARCH 31 1985

MADISON SQUARE GARDEN

THIS WAS THE ULTIMATE GAMBLE FOR JUNIOR. IF HIS "WRESTLEMANIA" THING FELL FLAT, THE COMPANY MIGHT NOT BE ABLE TO RECOUP THEIR LOSSES.

I'LL SAY THIS FOR VINCE JR., HE CERTAINLY KNEW HOW TO PULL OUT ALL THE STOPS IN THE QUEST FOR SUCCESS.

LIBERACE WAS THE GUEST TIMEKEEPER AND DANCED WITH THE ROCKETTES IN THE MIDDLE OF THE RING. NEVER IN MY WILDEST DREAMS DID I THINK I'D SEE SOMETHING LIKE THAT AT A WRESTLING SHOW!

I WAS INVOLVED IN A BODY SLAM CHALLENGE AGAINST MY LATEST ENEMY: BIG JOHN STUDD, MANAGED BY BOBBY "THE BRAIN" HEENAN. THE STIPULATION WAS SIMPLE, WHOMEVER SLAMMED THEIR OPPONENT FIRST WALKED OUT WITH $15,000!

I SLAMMED STUDD AND DECIDED TO TOSS THE CASH OUT TO THE CROWD. MUCH TO THE CHAGRIN OF HEENAN.

THE MAIN EVENT WAS EPIC... HOGAN AND HOLLYWOOD SUPERSTAR MR. T. VS. RODDY PIPER AND "MR. WONDERFUL" PAUL ORNDORFF.

THE PEOPLE LOVED WRESTLEMANIA. THE WWF BECAME A TRUE ENTERTAINMENT OPTION FOR MILLIONS OF VIEWERS ACROSS THE WORLD.

AFTER WRESTLEMANIA, TIME SEEMED TO MOVE FASTER WHILE MY BODY BEGAN TO GO A LOT SLOWER.

I COULD BARELY STAND... MY BACK, MY LEGS, MY JOINTS... *EVERYTHING* HURT ALL OF THE TIME.

AT WRESTLEMANIA 2 I PARTICIPATED IN A BATTLE ROYAL WITH A BUNCH OF WRESTLERS AND NFL PLAYERS.

I WON.

WWF WRESTLERS WERE SUPPOSED TO EXIST IN A WORLD CREATED BY VINCE JUNIOR. NO "OUTSIDE" CONTACTS OR CONNECTIONS TO GUYS FROM OTHER COMPANIES.

I DIDN'T CARE ABOUT THAT AND WHENEVER I GOT THE CHANCE TO TOUR DOWN SOUTH, I'D REACH OUT TO MY OLD CREW, ESPECIALLY DUSTY RHODES. THAT MAN COULD CHARM THE SPOTS OFF OF A LEOPARD IF YOU GAVE HIM THE CHANCE.

I LOVED HIS SING-SONG, FUNKY, SOUTHERN DRAWL.

ANDRE...

...YOU AIN'T LOOKIN' GOOD BROTHER.

I DON'T FEEL GOOD. I DON'T KNOW HOW MANY DAYS I GOT LEFT.

IN WRASSLIN'? THIS DON'T LAST FOREVER BABY.

MY LIFE. I FEEL MY DAYS ARE GETTING SHORT. MY BODY... THIS PAIN IS KILLING ME.

I SAID YOU DON'T LOOK GOOD, I DIDN'T SAY YOU WAS A DEAD MAN WALKIN'. WHAT YOU NEED?

ANOTHER DRINK.

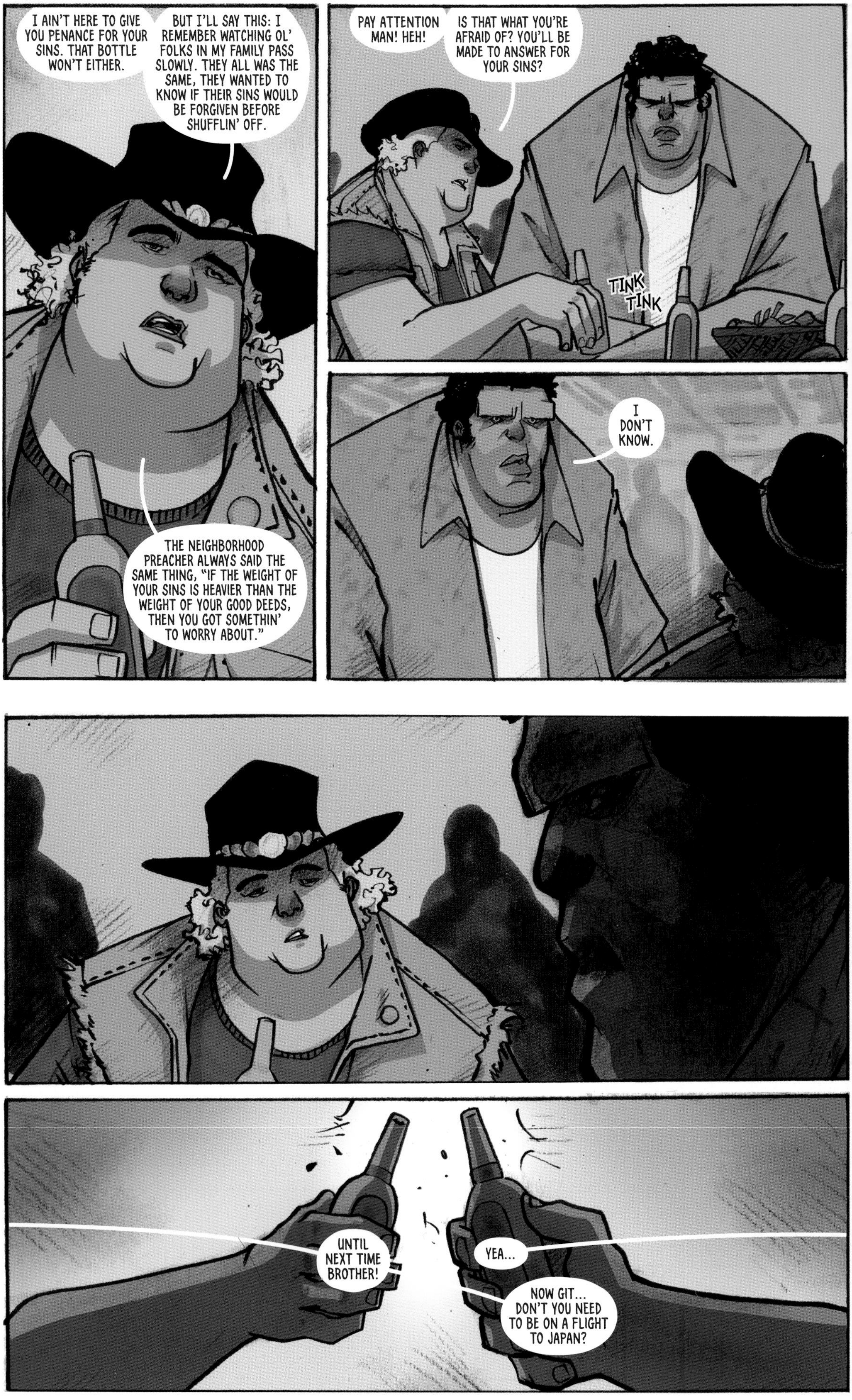

I AIN'T HERE TO GIVE YOU PENANCE FOR YOUR SINS. THAT BOTTLE WON'T EITHER.
BUT I'LL SAY THIS: I REMEMBER WATCHING OL' FOLKS IN MY FAMILY PASS SLOWLY. THEY ALL WAS THE SAME, THEY WANTED TO KNOW IF THEIR SINS WOULD BE FORGIVEN BEFORE SHUFFLIN' OFF.
THE NEIGHBORHOOD PREACHER ALWAYS SAID THE SAME THING, "IF THE WEIGHT OF YOUR SINS IS HEAVIER THAN THE WEIGHT OF YOUR GOOD DEEDS, THEN YOU GOT SOMETHIN' TO WORRY ABOUT."
PAY ATTENTION MAN! HEH!
IS THAT WHAT YOU'RE AFRAID OF? YOU'LL BE MADE TO ANSWER FOR YOUR SINS?
TINK
TINK
I DON'T KNOW.
UNTIL NEXT TIME BROTHER!
YEA...
NOW GIT... DON'T YOU NEED TO BE ON A FLIGHT TO JAPAN?

I'D BEEN BOOKED BY ANTONIO INOKI TO WRESTLE ONE OF HIS BIGGEST STARS IN NJPW - A LOUD-MOUTHED TOUGH GUY NAMED AKIRA MAEDA. AKIRA HAD MADE A NAME FOR HIMSELF BY FIGHTING IN A UNIQUE STYLE THAT COMBINED REAL MARTIAL ARTS WITH PRO WRESTLING MANEUVERS.

WHAT REALLY CEMENTED HIM AS A STAR WAS HIS OPEN HATRED FOR "REGULAR" PRO WRESTLERS. HE FELT WE WERE "WEAK" AND EASILY BEATEN.

MAY 26 1986

NATURALLY, THEY PUT HIM IN THE RING WITH ME.

THIS GUY BOTHERED ME. SO I DECIDED TO TEACH HIM A LESSON ABOUT REGULAR PRO WRESTLERS.

I REFUSED TO COOPERATE WITH THE PLANNED ACTION OF THE MATCH. I DIDN'T PULL MY PUNCHES WITH HIM.

SLOWLY BUT SURELY, HE LOST PATIENCE WITH ME... AND I WAS FINE WITH THAT.

WHAP!

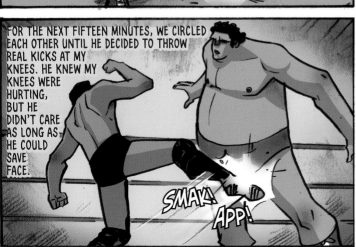

FOR THE NEXT FIFTEEN MINUTES, WE CIRCLED EACH OTHER UNTIL HE DECIDED TO THROW REAL KICKS AT MY KNEES. HE KNEW MY KNEES WERE HURTING, BUT HE DIDN'T CARE AS LONG AS HE COULD SAVE FACE.

SMAK! APP!

I WAS TIRED OF HIM. I LAID DOWN ON THE MAT AND TOLD HIM TO PIN ME.

AKIRA WASN'T STUPID, HE KNEW THAT THE MINUTE I GOT MY HANDS ON HIM, HE'D REGRET IT FOR THE REST OF HIS LIFE. SO HE DID THE SMART THING...

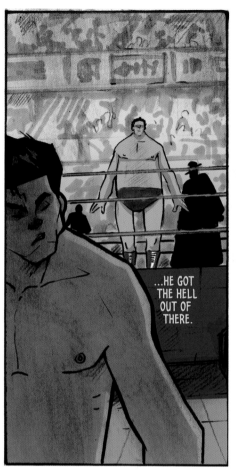

...HE GOT THE HELL OUT OF THERE.

THERE WERE DAYS WHEN I HATED OPENING MY EYES... ALL I HAD TO LOOK FORWARD TO WERE TWELVE HOURS OF TORTURE.

AND SOMETIMES THE LAUGHTER OF A CHILD COULD MAKE IT ALL DISAPPEAR.

VINCE JUNIOR HAD A DAUGHTER NAMED STEPHANIE.

I CALLED HER MY "LITTLE ANGEL" AND I THINK I SUBSTITUTED STEPHANIE FOR MY LOST RELATIONSHIP WITH ROBIN.

HOW'S MY LITTLE ANGEL?

GIGGLE

I FELL IN LOVE WITH THAT LITTLE GIRL, SHE NEVER ONCE SHOWED AN OUNCE OF FEAR WHEN WE FIRST MET.

THERE WERE GROWN MEN WHO COULDN'T MAKE THAT CLAIM.

THEY WANT ME TO PLAY A GIANT? I THINK I CAN DO THAT. WHAT'S THE NAME-? *THE PRINCESS BRIDE?* HEH!

THEN I GOT A CALL ABOUT APPEARING IN A FAIRY TALE MOVIE. IT PIQUED MY INTEREST.

I LAUGHED AT THE TITLE, BUT THE MOVIE TURNED OUT TO BE A MASTERPIECE THAT MIXED ADVENTURE, COMEDY, ROMANCE, AND INCREDIBLE SWORD FIGHTING.

I HAD A FANTASTIC TIME WITH THE OTHER ACTORS... MANDY, CARY, WALLACE...

I GOT ALONG FAMOUSLY WITH DIRECTOR ROB REINER AS WELL.

I DID WHATEVER THEY ASKED OF ME... DESPITE THE FACT THAT I COULD BARELY WALK.

AND THEN THERE WAS THE BEAUTIFUL YOUNG LADY WHO PLAYED THE PRINCESS...

ROBIN WRIGHT.

IF SHE ONLY KNEW HOW DELIGHTFUL HER NAME SOUNDED IN MY EARS.

WE FILMED IN ENGLAND DURING THE WINTER MONTHS. NOT THE BEST EXPERIENCE FOR THOSE NOT ACCUSTOMED TO THE EUROPEAN CHILL. ESPECIALLY FOR A GIRL RAISED IN SOUTHERN CALIFORNIA.

YOU OKAY, ROBIN?

Y-Y-YES... TRYING TO STAY WARM, I'M OKAY EXCEPT MY HEAD IS FREEZING.

AND THAT'S HOW YOU GET SICK. LET ME HELP.

FEEL BETTER?

ACTUALLY... YES. I DO. THANK YOU, ANDRE.

AFTER THE PRODUCTION WRAPPED, I COULDN'T TAKE THE PAIN ANYMORE. I REACHED OUT TO THE BEST BACK PHYSICIANS IN THE WORLD AND WAS SENT TO LONDON'S CROMWELL HOSPITAL. THEY NEEDED TO CUT MY BACK OPEN AND WIDEN MY SPINE OR ELSE I WOULDN'T BE ABLE TO WALK, LET ALONE WRESTLE EVER AGAIN.

I HAD TO WAIT ABOUT NINETY DAYS BEFORE THEY COULD OPERATE.

THEY NEEDED TO CONSTRUCT A LARGER BED, BIGGER SURGICAL TOOLS AND THEY EVEN BROUGHT A SMALL CRANE JUST IN CASE THEY HAD TO MOVE ME DURING THE DELICATE PROCEDURE.

MR. ROUSSIMOFF... WHAT ELSE WOULD YOU LIKE?

BEER.

THE SURGERY WAS A SUCCESS, BUT I WOULD NEED A WHILE TO FULLY RECUPERATE. IN THE MEANTIME, I GOT TO SEE MY FAMILY MEMBERS, INCLUDING MY NIECES AND NEPHEWS. SUDDENLY, MY WORLD DIDN'T FEEL SO EMPTY.

NOW I'M COMFORTABLE.

WE'VE ALREADY BROKEN MULTIPLE HEALTH CODES TO BRING YOU ALCOHOL, NOW TELL ME WHAT ELSE WOULD MAKE YOU COMFORTABLE?

BEER.

SERIOUSLY?

MORE BEER.

THROUGH THE MID-1980S, HULK HOGAN BECAME SYNONYMOUS WITH THE WORD "WRESTLING."

PEOPLE WHO DIDN'T EVEN WATCH WWF PROGRAMS KNEW EVERYTHING ABOUT THE MAN. IT WAS UNPRECEDENTED.

NO, YOU HAVEN'T. NOT TO ME, AND NOT TO THESE FANS. YOU'VE GOT TO UNDERSTAND SOMETHING, THERE'S ABOUT A MILLION NEW FANS WHO BELIEVE WE'VE ONLY EXISTED SINCE 1984. NOTHING BEFORE 1984 MATTERS TO THEM. I CAN CONTROL THEIR PERCEPTIONS AND WITH THAT CONTROL, WE CAN HIT A HOME RUN.

I'VE GOT AN IDEA FOR WRESTLEMANIA III.

YOU. HOGAN. ALL THE MARBLES.

I'VE ALREADY WRESTLED HOGAN... A BUNCH OF TIMES.

WHAT DO YOU NEED ME TO DO? I'M TIRED, BOSS.

HOGAN'S RUN OUT OF OPPONENTS. REMEMBER BACK WHEN YOU WERE IN MONTREAL?

WE'VE HAD EVERY MATCH COMBINATION WE CAN HAVE UNTIL WE DEVELOP THE NEXT GROUP OF BELIEVABLE CHALLENGERS.

YOU WON'T HAVE TO PERFORM UNTIL WRESTLEMANIA. WE'LL FLY YOU OUT TO CONNECTICUT AND YOU CAN TRAIN IN MY PERSONAL GYM. I KNOW STEPHANIE WOULD LOVE TO HAVE YOU AROUND AGAIN.

I BOOKED THE PONTIAC SILVERDOME IN MICHIGAN. NINETY-THREE THOUSAND SEATS. I'VE GOT TO FILL THOSE SEATS, MAN. WHAT DO YOU SAY?

WHERE'S IT GONNA BE?

VINCE'S PLAN WAS BRILLIANT. I'D NEVER BEEN THE "BAD GUY" IN THE UNITED STATES SO THE BIG TURN WOULD SHOCK FANS, PARTICULARLY THE LITTLE KIDS THAT LOOKED UP TO ME.

SO HE CONCOCTED AN ANGLE FOR ME TO CHALLENGE HOGAN... WHILE MAKING THE FANS HATE ME.

I'D APPROACHED HOGAN ON THE PIPER'S PIT SEGMENT OF THE WWF TV SHOW... WITH HOGAN'S ETERNAL NEMESIS BOBBY "THE BRAIN" HEENAN. YOU COULD HEAR THE FANS MURMUR IN CONFUSION ALONGSIDE HOGAN.

THEN I SAID HE DIDN'T RESPECT ME ENOUGH TO GIVE ME A TITLE SHOT EVEN THOUGH I'D BEEN "UNDEFEATED" MY ENTIRE CAREER. I DEMANDED A SHOT THEN AND THERE.

AND TO SHOW HOW SERIOUS I WAS, I RIPPED HIS "HULKAMANIA" SHIRT OFF HIS CHEST, UNKNOWINGLY DRAWING BLOOD WHEN HIS CRUCIFIX CUT INTO HIS SKIN.

IT WAS MARVELOUS.

THERE HAVE ONLY BEEN A FEW MOMENTS IN MY LIFE WHERE I'VE HAD MY BREATH TAKEN AWAY.

THIS PLACE MADE ME FEEL SMALL. FOR THE FIRST TIME IN MY ADULT LIFE, I FELT SMALL.

I'D HEARD THAT THE FANS HAD BEEN LINING UP OUTSIDE FROM THE CRACK OF DAWN. BY GOD, IT LOOKED LIKE VINCE HAD DONE IT.

THE FANS HATED ME.

YOU COULD TASTE THE ANGER, RESENTMENT, THE BETRAYAL IN THEIR HEARTS.

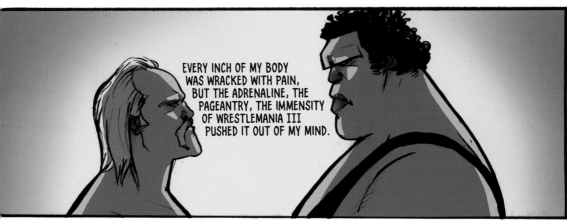

EVERY INCH OF MY BODY WAS WRACKED WITH PAIN, BUT THE ADRENALINE, THE PAGEANTRY, THE IMMENSITY OF WRESTLEMANIA III PUSHED IT OUT OF MY MIND.

THOK!

TO TEASE THE CROWD, WE'D DECIDED HOGAN WOULD ATTEMPT A BODY SLAM IN THE EARLY MOMENTS.

DIDN'T HAPPEN.

I'D DOMINATE MOST OF THE MATCH...

WHAM!!!

...BUILDING TOWARD THE INEVITABLE MOMENT WHEN HOGAN WOULD MOUNT HIS COMEBACK.

JUST LIKE I USED TO DO BACK IN THE OLD DAYS.

THUD!!!

NOW, FOR THE COUP DE GRACE... THE *BIG BOOT!*

IN JUNIOR'S LEGEND, I'D NEVER BEEN KNOCKED OFF MY FEET.

WHOOOOM!

WHOOOOOOOOM!!!

IT WAS THE LOUDEST NOISE I'D EVER HEARD IN MY LIFE.

ALL 93,173 OF THAT RECORD-BREAKING CROWD SHOUTED AT THE TOP OF THEIR LUNGS.

1- 2- 3!!!!

I'D DONE MY PART. I'D HANDED MY LEGACY TO HOGAN. WHATEVER IT IS I'D DONE FOR THE BUSINESS WOULD NOW BE PLACED IN HIS CAPABLE HANDS.

THERE WAS NO BIGGER STAGE THAN WRESTLEMANIA III. IF I TURNED MY BACK ON THE INDUSTRY AT THAT MOMENT, I'D BE SATISFIED WITH WHAT I'D ACCOMPLISHED.

OUR FEUD WAS FAR TOO HOT TO KILL. WE'D CONTINUE TO BATTLE THROUGHOUT THE YEAR. WE SET TELEVISION RECORDS WITH OUR REMATCH ON "SATURDAY NIGHT'S MAIN EVENT."

WE'D EVEN HAD A THIRD MAJOR FIGHT IN THE WORLD TITLE TOURNAMENT AT WRESTLEMANIA IV.

I EVEN HAD A NICE FEUD WITH JAKE "THE SNAKE" ROBERTS BASED UPON MY INTENSE FEAR OF THE REPTILES.

MY SPINE CONTINUED TO COMPRESS UPON ITSELF AND THERE WAS NOTHING ANYONE COULD DO. I WAS IN SUCH TREMENDOUS PAIN THAT I COULDN'T WALK AFTER MY MATCHES.

ALL THAT WAS LEFT WAS FOR ME TO WAIT UNTIL MY BODY COMPLETELY SHUT DOWN.

AND DULL THE PAIN.

I SPENT MORE AND MORE TIME AT MY RANCH IN ELLERBE, NORTH CAROLINA.

I HAD A SPECIAL CHAIR BUILT FOR ME BECAUSE MY FAVORITE ACTIVITY HAD BECOME SITTING.

I COULD FEEL THE DARKNESS CREEPING IN FROM THE SIDES, LIKE HOW WATER SNEAKS INTO GOGGLES IN A DEEP SWIMMING POOL.

THERE WAS A PART OF ME THAT WAS AFRAID. NO MATTER HOW MUCH PAIN I WAS IN, I DIDN'T WANT TO DIE.

I'D DONE SO MUCH, AND FELT THAT THERE WAS SO MUCH MORE TO SEE AND EXPERIENCE.

JANUARY 1993

I WAS AFRAID THAT MY SINS FAR OUTWEIGHED MY GOOD DEEDS. I WONDERED IF ROTTEN KHARMA WAS WAITING FOR ME ON THE OTHER SIDE.

WHEN I PICKED UP THE PHONE, I LEARNED THAT MY FATHER BORIS DIDN'T HAVE MUCH TIME LEFT. I NEEDED TO GET TO FRANCE BEFORE IT WAS TOO LATE.

RRRRRRRRRNNNNNGGGG

AU REVOIR, PAPA.

I CHECKED INTO A HOTEL IN PARIS BUT SPENT MOST OF MY TIME NEAR MY OLD FARMING COMMUNITY.

I'D FORGOTTEN HOW MUCH I'D MISSED MY FRIENDS FROM THE OLD DAYS... THESE WERE THE PEOPLE THAT DIDN'T JUDGE ME... WHO COULD FINISH MY SENTENCES... WHO GOT ALL MY JOKES WITHOUT EXPLANATION.

THAT ELUSIVE FEELING OF HAPPINESS CAME BACK IN FULL FORCE. I'D HAD A REALIZATION ABOUT WHAT LIFE WAS REALLY ABOUT...

...I'D SPENT MOST OF MY LIFE WONDERING WHY I'D BEEN CURSED WITH MY LARGE SIZE, I'D FROWNED BECAUSE I COULDN'T HAVE A NORMAL EXISTENCE.

BUT WHAT IF I WAS SENT HERE TO PROVIDE HAPPINESS FOR OTHERS?

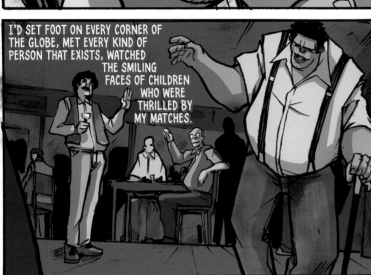

I'D SET FOOT ON EVERY CORNER OF THE GLOBE, MET EVERY KIND OF PERSON THAT EXISTS, WATCHED THE SMILING FACES OF CHILDREN WHO WERE THRILLED BY MY MATCHES.

I'D EARNED THE RESPECT OF DIGNITARIES, CELEBRITIES, AND MY FELLOW WRESTLERS.

MOST PEOPLE DON'T GET THE CHANCE TO LIVE ONE "ANDRE THE GIANT" YEAR. I LIVED THROUGH FORTY-SIX OF THEM.

MY LIFE WASN'T SO BAD AFTER ALL.

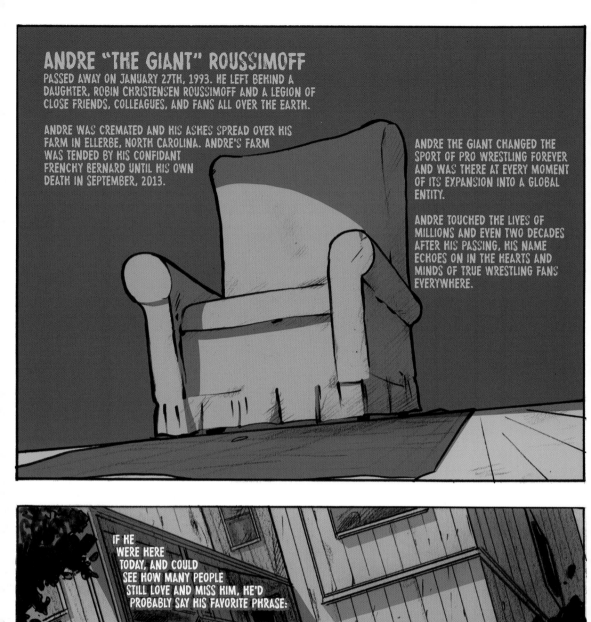

ANDRE "THE GIANT" ROUSSIMOFF

PASSED AWAY ON JANUARY 27TH, 1993. HE LEFT BEHIND A DAUGHTER, ROBIN CHRISTENSEN ROUSSIMOFF AND A LEGION OF CLOSE FRIENDS, COLLEAGUES, AND FANS ALL OVER THE EARTH.

ANDRE WAS CREMATED AND HIS ASHES SPREAD OVER HIS FARM IN ELLERBE, NORTH CAROLINA. ANDRE'S FARM WAS TENDED BY HIS CONFIDANT FRENCHY BERNARD UNTIL HIS OWN DEATH IN SEPTEMBER, 2013.

ANDRE THE GIANT CHANGED THE SPORT OF PRO WRESTLING FOREVER AND WAS THERE AT EVERY MOMENT OF ITS EXPANSION INTO A GLOBAL ENTITY.

ANDRE TOUCHED THE LIVES OF MILLIONS AND EVEN TWO DECADES AFTER HIS PASSING, HIS NAME ECHOES ON IN THE HEARTS AND MINDS OF TRUE WRESTLING FANS EVERYWHERE.

IF HE WERE HERE TODAY, AND COULD SEE HOW MANY PEOPLE STILL LOVE AND MISS HIM, HE'D PROBABLY SAY HIS FAVORITE PHRASE:

"THANKS, BOSS..."

FIN.

WRESTLING

PRESENTING THE WORLD'S LEADING WRESTLING STARS

WRITTEN BY

BRANDON "EASTSIDE" EASTON

ILLUSTRATED BY

DENIS "MAD DOG" MEDRI

EDITED BY

SHANNON "THE CANNON" DENTON

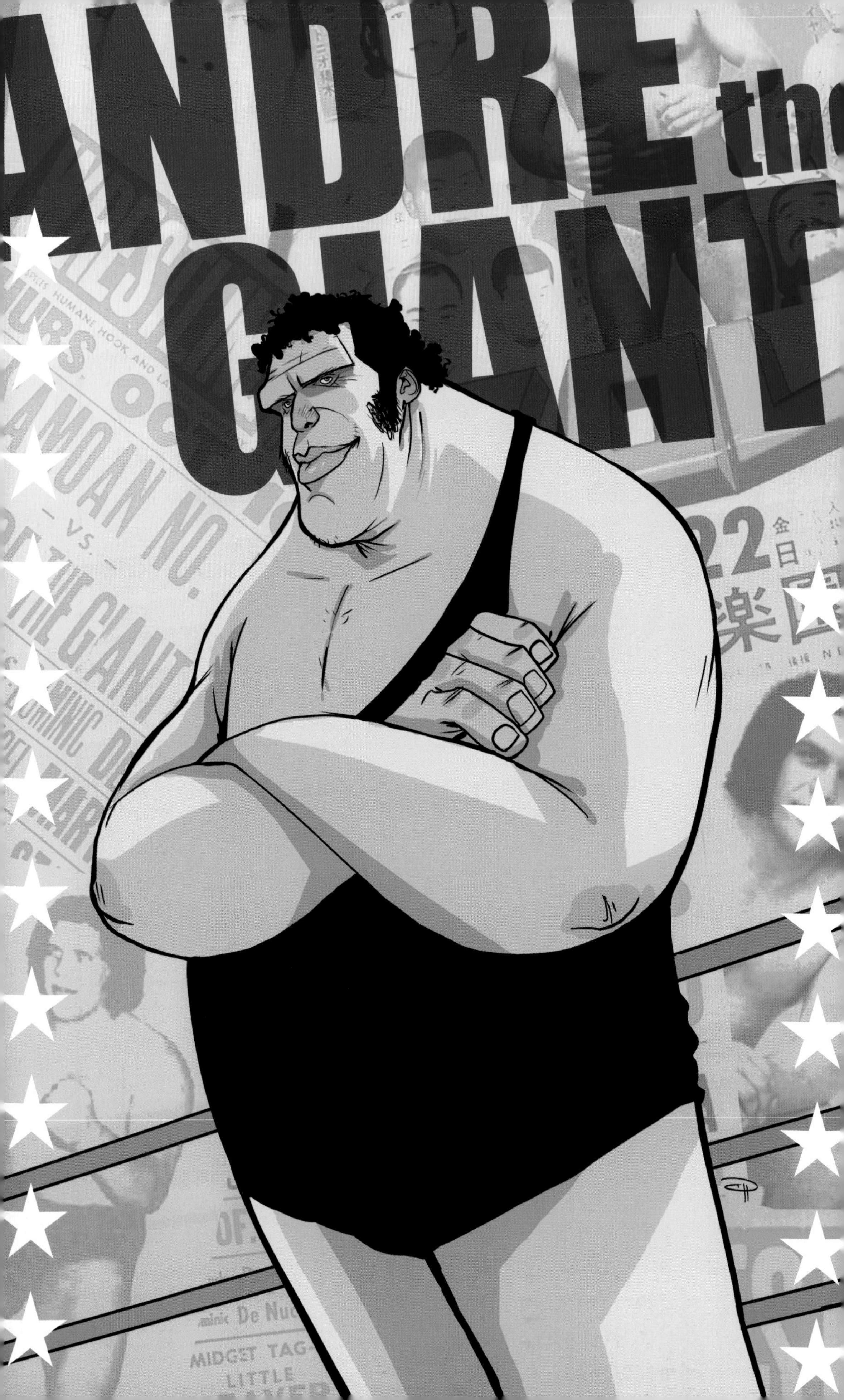
ANDRE th
HUMANE HOOK AND
SAMOAN NO.
— VS. —
THE GIANT
22
金
日
楽
De Nuc
MIDGET TAG-
LITTLE

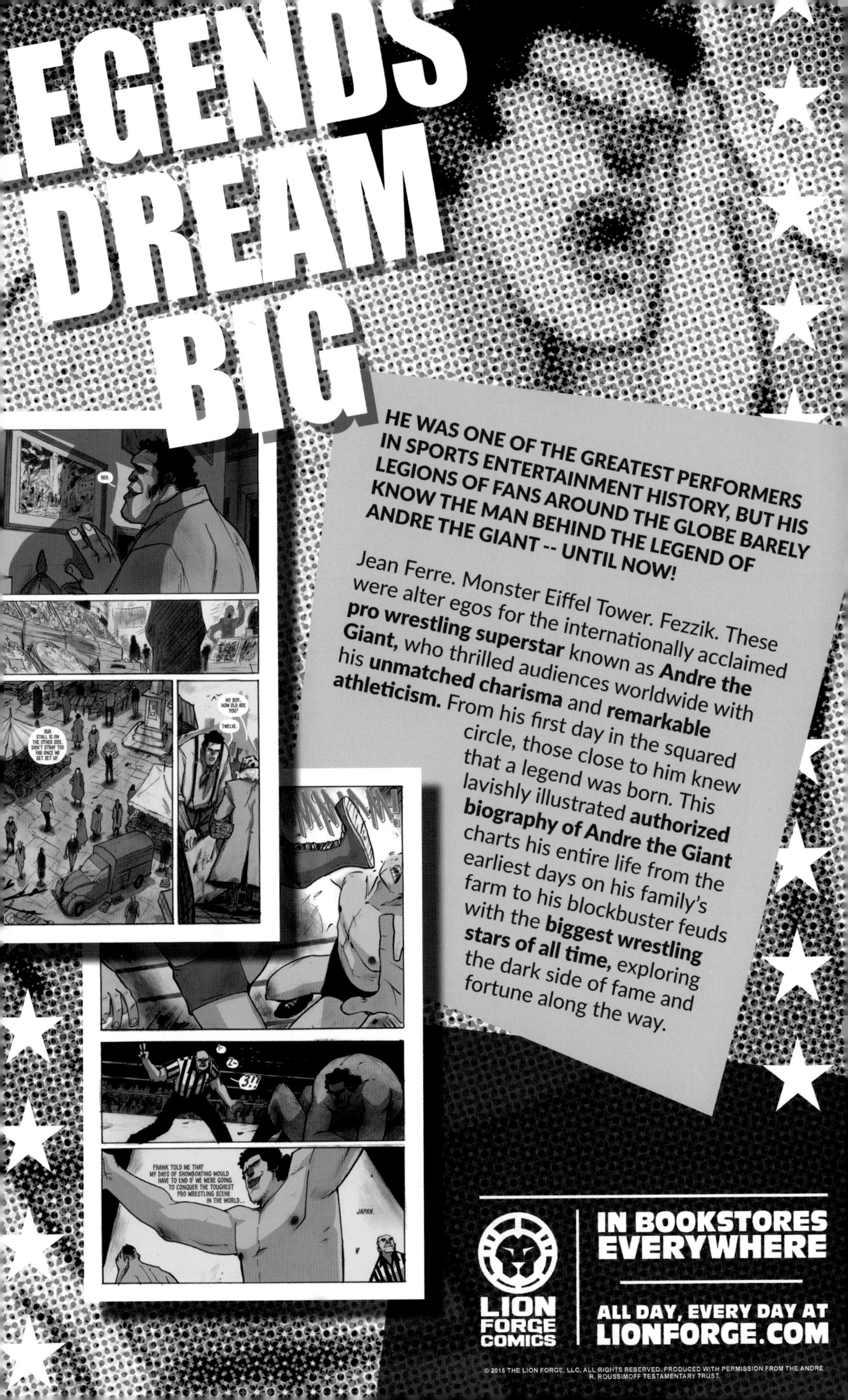
LEGENDS DREAM BIG
MEH.
OUR STALL IS ON THE OTHER SIDE. DON'T STRAY TOO FAR ONCE WE GET SET UP.
MY BOY, HOW OLD ARE YOU?
TWELVE.
1-
2-
3!!
FRANK TOLD ME THAT MY DAYS OF SHOWBOATING WOULD HAVE TO END IF WE WERE GOING TO CONQUER THE TOUGHEST PRO WRESTLING SCENE IN THE WORLD...
JAPAN.
HE WAS ONE OF THE GREATEST PERFORMERS IN SPORTS ENTERTAINMENT HISTORY, BUT HIS LEGIONS OF FANS AROUND THE GLOBE BARELY KNOW THE MAN BEHIND THE LEGEND OF ANDRE THE GIANT -- UNTIL NOW!
Jean Ferre. Monster Eiffel Tower. Fezzik. These were alter egos for the internationally acclaimed **pro wrestling superstar** known as **Andre the Giant,** who thrilled audiences worldwide with his **unmatched charisma** and **remarkable athleticism.** From his first day in the squared circle, those close to him knew that a legend was born. This lavishly illustrated **authorized biography of Andre the Giant** charts his entire life from the earliest days on his family's farm to his blockbuster feuds with the **biggest wrestling stars of all time,** exploring the dark side of fame and fortune along the way.
LION FORGE COMICS
IN BOOKSTORES EVERYWHERE
ALL DAY, EVERY DAY AT LIONFORGE.COM
© 2015 THE LION FORGE, LLC, ALL RIGHTS RESERVED. PRODUCED WITH PERMISSION FROM THE ANDRE R. ROUSSIMOFF TESTAMENTARY TRUST.

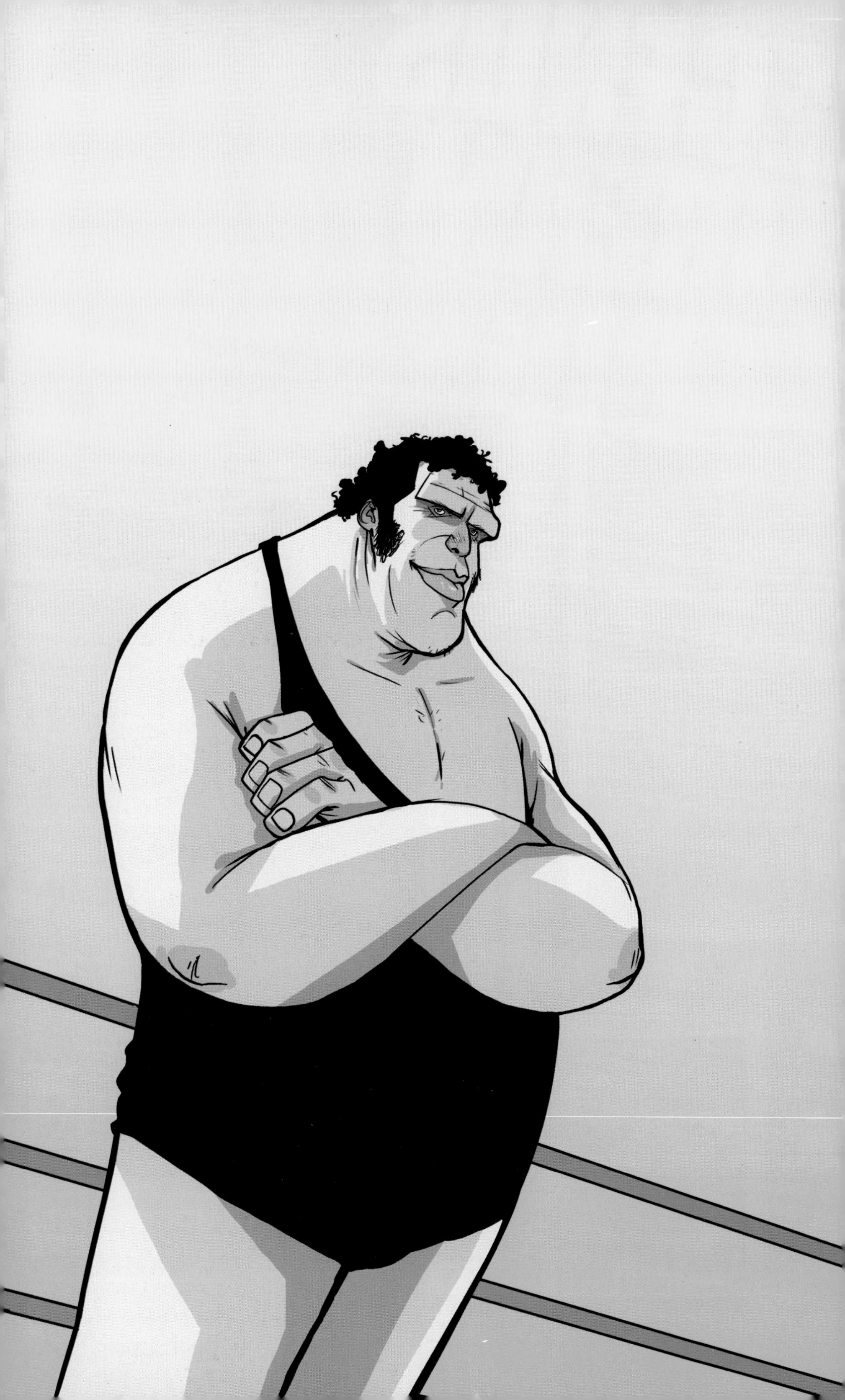